THE BIG SHOW

The Big Show

NEW ZEALANDERS,
D-DAY AND THE WAR IN EUROPE

EDITED BY ALISON PARR

AUCKLAND UNIVERSITY PRESS
IN ASSOCIATION WITH THE MINISTRY FOR CULTURE AND HERITAGE

First published 2006

Auckland University Press
University of Auckland
Private Bag 92019
Auckland
New Zealand
www.auckland.ac.nz/aup

ISBN-10: 1 86940 365 7
ISBN-13: 978 1 86940 365 2

National Library of New Zealand Cataloguing-in-Publication Data
The big show : New Zealanders, D-Day and the war in Europe /
edited by Alison Parr.
Includes bibliographical references and index.
ISBN-13: 978-1-86940-365-2
ISBN-10: 1-86940-365-7
1. World War, 1939-1945 — Campaigns — France — Normandy —
Personal narratives, New Zealand. 2. World War, 1939-1945 —
Personal narratives, New Zealand. I. Parr, Alison. II. Title.
940.548193–dc 22

COVER DESIGN: Christine Hansen
COVER IMAGE: Panel 13 of the Overlord Embroidery, from the D-Day Museum, Portsmouth, UK.
Courtesy of Portsmouth Museums & Records Services. www.ddaymuseum.co.uk

Printed by Printlink Ltd, Wellington

This book is dedicated to all New Zealanders
who lost their lives in the war in Europe, 1939–1945

Contents

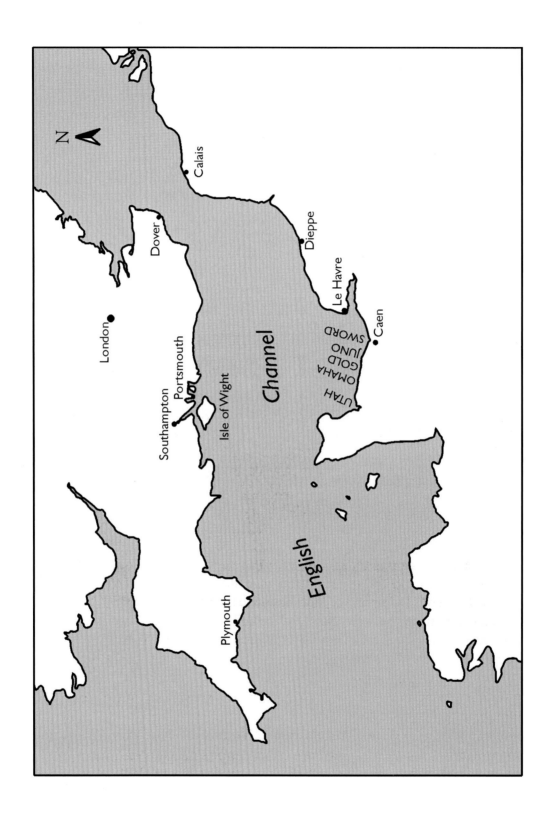

Foreword

HELEN CLARK, PRIME MINISTER

I am very pleased to welcome this book of personal accounts from New Zealanders who took part in the D-Day landings in 1944 and who helped end the war in Europe.

The Big Show is the first book produced from interviews conducted as part of the 'From Memory' war oral history project. This continues our recording of the voices of soldiers, sailors, airmen, nurses and other personnel who have served their country, at home and overseas, since the outbreak of the Second World War.

Oral histories give us a first-hand glimpse of the immensity of war. The landings on the Normandy beaches in June 1944 were certainly immense: there were over 150,000 Allied soldiers involved, and among those on the 6000 ships and 12,000 aircraft were 10,000 New Zealanders. Their part in the momentous D-Day landings which eventually brought an end to the Second World War is unknown to many of us. Here are home-grown perspectives of events which changed the world.

The stories in this book come from New Zealanders who served either in the RAF, including as pilots and navigators, or in the Royal Navy, including on the bridge of landing craft or as radar operators. Some of the men fought in, and were shot down from, the skies over France and Germany before D-Day. Their efforts continued for many months thereafter.

The Big Show is an important contribution to the Shared Memory Arrangement signed between New Zealand and France in 2004. Through the Arrangement, both countries are working to increase understanding and recognition of our shared experiences in the two world wars of the twentieth century. Not only do the stories in *The Big Show* take us to the beaches of Normandy, they also tell us of the extraordinarily brave French families who risked their lives to assist New Zealanders. I am particularly delighted that we were able to interview Mme Lucienne Vouzelaud, a former member of the French Resistance, whose actions ensured that one more New Zealander returned home from the war.

I acknowledge the kind assistance of France's Minister of Veterans' Affairs, M. Hamlaoui Mékachéra; His Excellency Jean-Michel Marlaud, Ambassador of France in Wellington; and the staff of the Ministère de la Défense in Paris and the French Embassy in New Zealand.

I thank the veterans who have so generously shared their stories with us. I congratulate Alison Parr and the team in the Ministry for Culture and Heritage for producing this book and undertaking the 'From Memory' project. I urge people to read *The Big Show* and learn more about the extraordinary, yet largely unknown, contribution of New Zealanders to the Normandy landings.

Helen Clark

HELEN CLARK
PRIME MINISTER

Foreword

FRENCH MINISTER OF VETERANS' AFFAIRS

HAMLAOUI MÉKACHÉRA,
FRENCH MINISTER OF VETERANS' AFFAIRS

France remembers New Zealand's commitment in the Second World War – in Europe, where thousands of New Zealanders were in service during D-Day operations in June, 1944, but also in the Pacific, where they fought magnificently for our common values.

That is why I am especially delighted about the publication of *The Big Show*. It is a strong and moving testimony: testimony to New Zealand airmen and sailors who entered into the torment of World War II with courage; testimony to the solidarity and bravery of the members of the French Resistance who came to their aid.

This book is a remarkable contribution to France and New Zealand's common heritage.

I wish to thank everyone involved: the various New Zealand and French departments, as well as our respective embassies in Paris and Wellington.

This book exemplifies the friendliness and mutual gratitude that character- ises the relations between France and New Zealand in war remembrance.

This initiative is one outcome of the Shared Memory Arrangement which I had the honour of signing with the New Zealand Prime Minister, Rt Hon. Helen Clark, on 5 June 2004, in order to facilitate research work between our two countries and to make known to the French and New Zealand public these pages from the history book that were written together.

I am very pleased to note that, up to the highest level, the New Zealand authorities are eager to promote and develop exchanges with us in the domain of the shared memory of twentieth-century wars.

It is in this same spirit that New Zealand has been invited to the first international conference on shared memory, which will be organised in Paris in October 2006.

If to remember is to evoke passion and suffering, it is also to share our memory with those peoples whose destinies have intersected with our own. This joint focus on our common past, the ties created between our peoples, will develop a sense of belonging to the same shared future.

We address, above all, the youth of our two countries. The younger generation must carry the legacy of yesterday's soldiers. They will be called upon to continue to promote the inestimable values of peace and freedom.

Side by side, as we were yesterday, France and New Zealand are resolutely committed to this path.

HAMLAOUI MÉKACHÉRA
MINISTER OF VETERANS' AFFAIRS

Acknowledgements

Just after the anniversary of D-Day in 2005, I made the ferry journey across the English Channel from Portsmouth to Caen. I had already recorded most of the interviews in this book, and the men who had shared their stories seemed very much with me. While other ferry passengers around me slept or read newspapers, I watched as the flat Normandy coast emerged from a grey haze. In my mind were two young New Zealanders, one from Petone and the other from Manawatu. More than 60 years before, thousands of miles from home, in the chaos of D-Day, both had struggled to land troops and tanks on the stretch of coast before me. Their stories are in this collection and, along with those of all the other veterans here, they affected me deeply. They brought D-Day and the war in Europe alive and enriched my understanding of that time. I know their memories will do the same for others – such is the power of oral history.

For this reason my greatest debt is to the veterans whose stories appear in this book. They have my sincere thanks for the trust, energy, and courage it took to delve back more than six decades and put what they remember on the record. It has been a privilege to work with each of them. I am grateful, too, for their hospitality, and that of their wives.

As the first step in this project, with valuable assistance from Veterans' Affairs New Zealand, we called on veterans of the RAF and RN during the war in Europe to complete questionnaires about their experience. We are grateful to all who responded to this call. Every completed questionnaire will be held in the Alexander Turnbull Library.

All the interviews in this collection are edited versions of hours of recorded material. The unedited copies of each interview, with their abstracts, will be archived in the Oral History Centre at the Alexander Turnbull Library, available for researchers in the future. My thanks go to Curator Linda Evans and her team for their work there.

In the Ministry for Culture and Heritage I am particularly grateful to Chief Historian Bronwyn Dalley for her consistently enthusiastic and intelligent leadership; General Editor War History Ian McGibbon for his willingness to share his knowledge of our military history; research librarian Fran McGowan for her initiative and efficiency; David Green for his skilled copy editing; Megan Hutching for sharing her experience in oral history; and Claire Taggart for her administrative support. I very much appreciate the encouragement and assistance of other colleagues in the History Group, and also of Henare Howard and Kerry Harvey.

The French Ambassador to New Zealand, His Excellency Jean-Michel Marlaud, and Louise Wetterström from the Cultural and Scientific Service of the French Embassy have supported this project from its inception and given valuable practical assistance for which I am grateful. It has been a pleasure to work with them. In France, my sincere thanks go to Madame Lucienne Vouzelaud in Brou, for her gracious and generous hospitality and her willingness to share memories of an extraordinary time in her life. For their hospitality and assistance, I am grateful to Richard Schneider and Christophe Thireau from the Direction de la Mémoire du Patrimoine et des Archives, Ministère de la Défense, Paris; I am also particularly grateful to Erwan le Gall, Assistant-Mémoire, Service Départemental de l'Eure-et-Loir de l'Office National des Anciens Combattants et Victimes de Guerre, in Chartres, for his ongoing practical support and interest in this project.

Others whose willing assistance I appreciate include Joan McCracken and her staff in the Photographic Collections of the Alexander Turnbull Library, Paul Restall at the Navy Museum, and Matthew O'Sullivan at the Air Force Museum. I am grateful to Elizabeth Caffin and her team at Auckland University Press, particularly designer Katrina Duncan. Thanks are also due to The Translation Service in Wellington, and to the Imperial War Museum in London. The D-Day Museum in Portsmouth, England generously allowed us to use an image from the Overlord Embroidery on the cover of this book.

Alison Parr
February 2006

Introduction

ALISON PARR

We knew the big show was coming. . . . This time, success was absolutely important. TREVOR MULLINDER, 487 (NZ) SQUADRON, RAF

YOUNG TREVOR MULLINDER FROM TAIHAPE WAS QUICK TO PICK UP ROYAL AIR Force slang. When his squadron was briefed on the eve of D-Day in June 1944, he knew it would be no ordinary 'show' – like everyone else involved, he recognised this as the most vital mission possible. The huge military machine that embarked on the invasion of France was designed to end the war in Europe and bring victory to the Allies. Failure was unthinkable.

Trevor is one of the thirteen New Zealanders whose memories are included here. This collection of their stories offers a glimpse of a momentous time in history, seen through the eyes of young men born and raised in places like Matamata and Invercargill – a home-grown perspective on a war on the other side of the world. Thousands of words have been written about D-Day and the war in Europe, thoroughly exploring the political, military and diplomatic aspects of those watershed years. This book contains a personal perspective on that time – the reminiscences and reflections of elderly men who have been prepared to recall some of the most painful and most exhilarating times of their lives. Oral history gives us access to this experience – to Eric Krull's perseverance in the midst of mayhem as he tended to a severely wounded man and landed tanks on a French beach, and to Terry Scott's joy in finding his mate Sid alive after their frigate was sunk in the English Channel. It enables us to share the impressions of Russell Clarke, who witnessed the impact of war on civilians in Holland, and the despair of Trevor Mullinder as he discovered the deathplace of hundreds of slave workers of the Third Reich in Germany.

At the time of D-Day and the last year of the war in Europe, troops of the Second New Zealand Division were battling their way up through Italy. Other New Zealanders in the Pacific were beginning to come home after seeing action in Solomon Islands. In the United Kingdom, 10,000 more New Zealanders were serving with the Royal Air Force and Royal Navy. Many of these men became witnesses to one of the largest amphibious landings in history – an action that coordinated land, sea and air forces for the invasion of France. Operation Overlord began before dawn on 6 June 1944, when more than 153,000 Allied soldiers left the south coast of England to cross the Channel. They made their journey in two groups, the larger in a vast armada that carried more than 130,000 of them to land on the beaches of Normandy. Ahead of them went hundreds of planes and gliders flying another 23,000 troops to drop zones inland – their role, to take strategic points and provide protection to the men landing on the beaches. Together, the two groups would begin to reclaim German-held territory. Over the next months, as further troops joined them, their number would grow to more than two million.

No New Zealand ground forces landed on the beaches of Normandy, but many New Zealand servicemen were on board the ships and planes that headed for France that stormy summer morning. Some were serving in the Royal Navy as seamen or officers on frigates, battleships and destroyers – men like Gordon Forrester, Jim Pollok and Terry Scott. Others, like Jack Ingham and Eric Krull, were in charge of landing craft, vessels that carried the troops and tanks to the invasion. Above them flew men like Don Sisley with Royal Air Force crews in Dakotas and gliders, carrying paratroops. Russell Clarke, Trevor Mullinder and Philip Stewart set out in fighter planes on operations in support of the landings, while RAF bombers sent to attack enemy defences were crewed by men like George Wirepa. Unusual tasks fell to other New Zealanders on D-Day – with his elite bomber squadron, Les Munro was assigned to create a sophisticated deception further up the French coast, while Ned Hitchcock, an electrical engineer with RAF coastal radar, joined an American unit landing vital equipment on Omaha Beach.

On deck

The New Zealanders who took part in D-Day and the final months of the war in Europe had arrived in the United Kingdom over the previous four years. By 1944 more than 4700 of them were serving in Royal Navy ships. Some had joined the navy at the outbreak of war because they loved the sea. Others had chosen this service because they saw it as promising a less personal war than they would have had to fight in the army. And then there were those who simply grasped the promise of travel and adventure.

The Royal Naval Volunteer Reserve march past soldiers of the Second Echelon of 2NZEF in Wellington, April 1940. WAR HISTORY COLLECTION, ALEXANDER TURNBULL LIBRARY, 1/4-049242-G

They had found their way into the navy through a number of recruiting schemes. The most common, Scheme B, was for ordinary seamen aged between twenty and 30 years. This also offered potential for selection as officers, which attracted men like Eric Krull. Other schemes recruited volunteers for specific skills – people like telegraphist Jack Ingham and radar operator Jim Pollok. These recruits of the Royal New Zealand Naval Volunteer Reserve (RNZNVR) were enlisted for 'Hostilities Only' and were 'loaned' to the Royal Navy after a short period of training in New Zealand.

There were no Royal New Zealand Navy ships at the Normandy landings, but the *Monowai* and *Aorangi*, both from the New Zealand merchant navy, took their place in the D-Day armada. The *Monowai* was fitted out as a troopship and after the invasion continued transporting reinforcements to France. *Aorangi* played a role as a depot ship for the dozens of tugs that towed the artificial Mulberry Harbours across the Channel, and later helped to get casualties back to England. While

New Zealand seaman Terry Scott managed to swim to safety after his ship, HMS *Lawford*, was sunk two days after D-Day, not all his countrymen were so fortunate. In the month after the landings ten young New Zealanders were killed when their destroyer, HMS *Isis*, was sunk by a mine while on an anti-submarine patrol off Normandy.

High flyers

For thousands of other young New Zealand men, the air force was their first choice. Like the navy, it offered the chance to serve without the risk of being involved in hand-to-hand combat, an appealing aspect for several of the men included in this book. For some, like fighter pilot Philip Stewart, this was the deciding factor: 'I had a horror of any form of warfare which was mainly thrusting bayonets through people.' As well, the 'boys in blue' carried a glamorous reputation and aircrew had the opportunity to learn to fly at a time when this was otherwise a remote possibility.

By 1944 more than 6000 New Zealanders were serving in the RAF in the United Kingdom. From the formation of the Royal New Zealand Air Force (RNZAF) in 1937, young men had been trained as officers at Wigram and posted for short stints to the RAF. As the Second World War loomed, the New Zealand government offered more airmen to the RAF, proposing to train 1000 pilots a year. When war was declared, the RNZAF was mobilised and volunteers were called for, to serve, for as long as the war lasted, in either the RNZAF or the RAF. By this time there were already 550 New Zealanders serving in the RAF, 200 of them in the United Kingdom and the others in India and the Middle East. Air combat costs lives, and the official RAF expectation of losses – or 'wastage', as it was termed – was huge. The forecast need for each year of the war was 20,000 pilots and 30,000 other crew. Unable to train this number itself, Britain asked the Commonwealth for help and the New Zealand government committed itself to providing the RAF with 880 fully-trained pilots each year, later increasing this number to more than 2000. Pilots had their first flying lessons at bases throughout the country, including Whenuapai, Palmerston North, Harewood, Wigram and Taieri. In all, more than 2700 pilots completed their training in New Zealand before heading for England and the RAF.

From April 1940, just over 7000 more New Zealanders sailed for Canada as part of the Empire Air Training Scheme, established to keep up the flow of aircrews from Commonwealth countries to the RAF. New Zealanders who trained there as pilots, navigators, wireless operators, air gunners and bomb aimers have vivid memories of this time. Many remember the vast expanses of Canadian landscape

By the middle of 1940 thousands of young New Zealand men had responded to appeals such as this to join the air force. WAR HISTORY COLLECTION, ALEXANDER TURNBULL LIBRARY, F 146816½

as they travelled by rail from Vancouver to Saskatchewan and later to the east coast for their departure. They enjoyed meals and outings with Canadian families – a few left behind Canadian girlfriends and fiancées. At the end of their time there, some New Zealand airmen returned to serve closer to home, in the Pacific, but most were destined for the United Kingdom. A common port of call before sailing across the Atlantic was New York, and the energy and vibrancy of that city left a lasting impression on young men who had grown up in places like Te Kuiti and Gisborne.

Once in England, the New Zealanders were posted to Operational Training Units (OTUs) before being assigned to squadrons. When they began their operational careers, their average age was 21. They would be expected to fly a 'tour' of 30 sorties, or combat flights, before being given time out. Assignment to a squadron and operational flying often ended a time of frustration – at last they could begin the job they had left New Zealand to do.

New Zealand airmen on leave in New York – time out between training in Canada and the war in Europe. WAR HISTORY COLLECTION, ALEXANDER TURNBULL LIBRARY, 17637¼

There were seven squadrons with a New Zealand identity in the RAF, manned largely by New Zealanders. Two of these were in Bomber Command (75 and 487), three in Fighter Command (485, 486, 488), and two in Coastal Command (489 and 490). A year before D-Day the Second Tactical Air Force (2 TAF) was formed within the RAF to give close support to the Allied armies as they advanced through France, Belgium and Holland. Four of the RAF's New Zealand squadrons were assigned to this force – three fighter and one bomber. Of these, Russell Clarke's 485 Squadron, flying fighter planes, was the first to operate from the continent of Europe, moving to France in August 1944. The commander of the Second Tactical Air Force was Air Vice-Marshal Arthur Coningham, who, although born in Australia, had been brought up in Wellington.

The majority of New Zealand airmen in the RAF were not in the New Zealand squadrons but flew alongside men from Canada, Australia, South Africa and the

United Kingdom. New Zealand was represented, at some stage, in almost all RAF squadrons, and during the months of the Normandy invasion New Zealanders served with both air and ground crews of the RAF in Bomber, Fighter, Coastal and Transport Commands.

Sirens and shelters

Jack Ingham from Petone recognised that 'we'd come to the war' when he arrived in Liverpool to the smell of burnt sugar from the Tate and Lyle warehouse, the result of a Luftwaffe attack on the docks the night before. He was one of many New Zealanders based in the United Kingdom from the time of the Blitz, when English cities were pounded nightly by German bombs.

The bombing of Liverpool and other British cities, especially London, was a consequence of the failure of German plans to invade the United Kingdom. From the time France capitulated to the Germans in June 1940, Hitler had talked about crossing the Channel and conquering the United Kingdom. In preparation for this

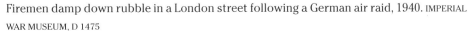

Firemen damp down rubble in a London street following a German air raid, 1940. IMPERIAL WAR MUSEUM, D 1475

Londoners sleeping in the Elephant and Castle Underground station during the Blitz, November 1940. IMPERIAL WAR MUSEUM, D 1568

he tried to gain control of the skies in what became known as the Battle of Britain. The Luftwaffe set out to defeat the RAF, attacking fighter planes in the air over southern England. At the same time, German bombers attacked British airfields. But in September they shifted their bombing to the city of London and within weeks the Blitz – from blitzkrieg, lightning war – had begun. From autumn 1940 until mid-May the following year, the Germans relentlessly bombed London and other cities, including Portsmouth, Plymouth, Bristol, Birmingham, Coventry and Liverpool. In the German arsenal were incendiary bombs that, instead of blowing up their targets, penetrated the roofs of buildings and started fires which spread rapidly.

When the air-raid sirens wailed, Jack Ingham and other Kiwi servicemen on leave in the capital joined Londoners in the Underground – its deep tunnels offering protection to thousands of people. Above ground, the New Zealanders saw first-hand the destruction of buildings and lives caused by the bombing. They also became aware of the extraordinary stoicism of the British people, who were determined not to concede defeat. It was a staunchness that impressed Jack – 'the fact that they weren't going to give in, weren't going to be beaten. It changed your whole attitude towards them.' During the Blitz 43,000 British civilians were killed and more than 130,000 injured, but Germany failed to force the United Kingdom into submission. Hitler's invasion of Britain would never take place, and within a year Allied leaders were preparing an invasion in the opposite direction.

The grand plan

From the time of the French defeat in 1940 Hitler feared an eventual Allied invasion in the west. A successful landing would not only stretch his resources, but also threaten his country's industrial centre – the Rhine-Ruhr region that produced the coal, iron and steel vital to Germany's war effort. Planning a defence against such an attack, Hitler declared himself 'the greatest fortress-builder of all time' as he created what became known as Fortress Europe. Building of the 'Atlantic Wall' – more than 2000 kilometres of concrete and steel coastal defences stretching from Denmark to the Spanish border – began in the summer of 1942. The Führer was right to worry about such an invasion. Allied planning began in earnest in 1943, and by February 1944 British and American military leaders had agreed on a joint plan – a complex strategy for a landing and the subsequent advance of thousands of Allied troops through France.

By the middle of 1944 German armed forces in Europe were stretched and struggling. Germany was losing the war in Italy, where New Zealand troops with the Second Division were among those who celebrated the fall of Rome on 4 June. In the Soviet Union the Germans had suffered major defeats at Stalingrad and Kursk. By late May 1944 the Russians were planning a major offensive that would shatter the German eastern front. As his forces battled in the east, Hitler appointed Field Marshal Rommel, known to New Zealand soldiers in North Africa for his role as commander of the Axis forces there, to be responsible for the build-up of defences along the French coast. It was Rommel's belief that an invasion had to be stopped on the beaches – if the Allies won a foothold, the war would be lost. To help thwart such a landing, the Atlantic Wall was strengthened with artillery, mines, barbed wire and other obstructions.

Armament personnel load an 8000lb bomb onto a Lancaster, Coningsby RAF station, 1943.
LES MUNRO COLLECTION

The shortest shipping distance from England to France across the Channel is just 34 kilometres, from Dover to Pas de Calais, where Rommel put his most powerful artillery. But the Allied leaders chose another landing place further south, nearly 160 kilometres from England. The strategic benefits offset the much greater distance. Not only was the coast of Normandy less strongly defended than the Pas de Calais area, but the large ports around Southampton and Portsmouth, directly across the Channel, were better able than more northern ports to cope with the colossal build-up of ships required. The stretch of the Normandy coast chosen as the invasion site was divided into five beaches, codenamed (from east to west) Sword, Juno, Gold, Omaha and Utah. The first three were the destination of British and Canadian troops, the remaining two of the Americans. The first wave of D-Day troops was to establish beachheads and then prepare to advance inland once follow-up forces arrived.

The overall campaign to open up a new Allied front in France was code-named Operation Overlord, while the naval operation to transport and land forces in Normandy was called Operation Neptune. The date chosen for the landings was known as D-Day in accordance with a common military convention – D stood for the day on which an operation was scheduled to take place. So, D–1 was the day before D-Day, while D+1 was the day after. The French called 6 June 1944 J-Jour.

The logistical planning for the entire operation was extraordinary. In order to get all the soldiers and their equipment on to the beaches of Normandy, more than 4000 transport ships were amassed. Many hundreds of these were built specifically for the invasion. Landing craft for tanks (LCT) and infantry (LCI) were manufactured in shipyards in the United Kingdom and on the east coast of America. Some of the latter were more luxurious than their British counterparts, as Jack Ingham discovered when he collected his first LCI in New York – it was equipped with 'beautiful American bits and pieces' such as an ice chest, a coffee-making machine and reading lamps in his officer's cabin.

Officers and men needed training in combined landings, and some gained experience in earlier assaults. Jack and his crew got their chance to learn the ropes in the Mediterranean and then, in the Allied invasion of Sicily, experienced the real thing, under fire from land and air. Eric Krull picked up his LCT from an English shipyard at Lowestoft and trained with his crew for nearly a year around the coast. They practised beaching their vessel, but, surprisingly, the first time they actually landed tanks on shore was on Gold Beach on D-Day.

Preparing the ground

Also readying itself for the invasion was the RAF, whose energy went into preparing occupied territory for the ground forces. Because German troops and equipment were transported mainly by train it was deemed necessary to destroy as much of the French rail system as possible to disrupt plans for reinforcement. Spitfire pilot Philip Stewart was one of many airmen in Fighter Command to go behind enemy lines well before D-Day, attacking strategic targets such as railway lines, troop trains and other transport. These attacks intensified in the build-up to the invasion.

Bomber Command was also paving the way for the invasion forces. At its head was Air Chief Marshal Sir Arthur Harris – known by this time as 'Bomber' Harris. In the two months leading up to D-Day, he turned his attention to railway targets in France and Belgium. German reports at the time wrote of the 'crippling' of the transport system. By D-Day, Normandy had been virtually isolated by the combined Allied fighter and bomber offensive. The destruction of railways and road communications prevented German reserve troops getting to Normandy during the landings and for some time afterwards. From April, as the build-up to the invasion intensified, strategic bombing also included targets such as military camps, arms factories in France and Belgium, and batteries and radar sites along the French coast.

Reducing the power of the Luftwaffe was also a primary goal at this time, and fighter squadrons flew systematic and debilitating attacks on German fighter airfields and planes on the ground in France, as well as waging battle in the air. RAF fighters destroyed nearly 2000 enemy aircraft over the English Channel and surrounding countryside. This, combined with the fact that the bulk of the Luftwaffe was busy on the eastern front fighting the Soviet air force, meant that by D-Day the Allies had supremacy in the skies around England and over the French coast.

Supporting acts

The intricate planning and preparation for the Allied move on France extended well beyond the actual landing. To sustain the invasion force after D-Day, continuing supplies of food, equipment and fuel would be essential. Helping to meet these needs, two audacious engineering projects were conceived and carried out.

One of these was the creation of PLUTO – Pipe Line Under the Ocean – to supply fuel to troops in France. Specially designed pipes were coiled around drums and run out from cable-laying ships. The first PLUTO ran along the bed of the Channel over the 100 kilometres from the Isle of Wight to Cherbourg. Other pipes laid later in the campaign delivered up to 18,000 litres of fuel a day.

The second major engineering feat completed in support of the Allied advance was the construction of what were code-named Mulberry Harbours – a complex system of temporary floating quays that would provide artificial harbours on the coast of Normandy until ports were in Allied hands. Because all the naval shipyards were fully occupied building landing craft, the huge concrete and steel structures were built in rivers and inlets around Britain. It took 20,000 workers just seven months to finish the job. In the wake of the armada, the Mulberries were towed across the Channel to form breakwaters for sheltering and unloading ships. Secrecy cloaked the Mulberry project, and Leading Seaman Terry Scott from Cromwell was one of many bemused by the constructions. 'We'd seen the huge concrete harbour blocks . . . . nobody knew what they were.' However, there were no doubts that they were to do with the long-awaited invasion – 'we thought things must be coming right'.

Gathering strength

While the Mulberry Harbours and PLUTO were in their final stages of construction, tens of thousands of troops were pouring into the area around Portsmouth and Southampton from all parts of the United Kingdom. Many more streamed across the Atlantic in transport ships and landing craft. By the end of May there were more than one and a half million Americans in the barracks and tent villages of southern England. Christchurch radar engineer Ned Hitchcock joined one of the American units just before D-Day and, after the austerity of the RAF rations he was used to, enjoyed the variety and richness of American food. The Americans approached warfare differently in other ways too – Ned was amused to be issued with two condoms in his kit for Normandy. Subsequent reports suggest that American troops used them to keep water and sand out of their rifle barrels.

As with any major military operation, secrecy was a key to the success of the D-Day landings – camouflage was extensively used on transport and equipment. From two weeks before D-Day the troop camps were sealed off. No one was allowed to leave or enter except in exceptional circumstances. There was also strict security around the docks and airfields of southern England, and all leave was cancelled.

Faking it

With such an obvious military concentration in one area, it was impossible to conceal from the Germans that an invasion was in preparation. As a counterpoint, a complex deception was under way, code-named Operation Fortitude. The idea behind the plot was to trick the enemy as to where and when the Allied forces would storm French beaches – to make them believe the landings would take place further up the French coast, at the narrowest part of the Channel in Pas de Calais. While forces built up around the real assembly areas of Portsmouth and Southampton, other collections of vehicles were moved to eastern England, where phoney radio messages, intercepted by the Germans, suggested assault divisions were massing.

The most elaborate part of the deception was the simulation of an invasion fleet by dummy landing craft assembled in eastern England. On the night before D-Day, other small flotillas of motorboats, fitted with radar equipment that made them seem much larger on enemy screens, headed across the Channel towards Calais. This fake flotilla was joined by Les Munro's 617 Squadron in their Lancasters, dropping bundles of 'Window' – reflective aluminium strips. On German radar the 'Window' created the impression of hundreds of ships headed for the decoy area and drew the enemy commanders' attention away from the real landing sites. At the time, the men of 617 Squadron were disappointed that their finely honed skills were not being used in direct attacks. As Les recalls, 'We had a very, very specific, very important role to play, but it was a very docile role.'

Operation Fortitude included other ingenious aspects – dummy paratroops, some fitted with explosives that sounded like gunfire, were dropped in places away from real target zones. These combined deceits were so successful that the Germans believed the real invasion was yet another diversion, and for several critical days after D-Day held back their reserve troops from the Normandy coast.

A question of timing

On the eve of D-Day an estimated two million men and half a million vehicles clogged southern England. In the water around Portsmouth and Southampton more than 6000 ships were assembled – including the 4000 landing craft carrying troops and equipment, and 1200 Royal Navy warships to support the landings. By this time, all servicemen knew they were heading for France. The question was, when?

Some of the thousands of landing craft assembling in Southampton before D-Day. IMPERIAL WAR MUSEUM, A 23731

The timing of D-Day was subject to a number of critical considerations, including the need for the tides to be suitable for landing craft to beach safely, and a full moon for the airborne troops. The day chosen, when the required conditions coincided, was 5 June. By that day every Allied serviceman had been briefed and was primed to go into action. However, the one thing that even the most stringent military planning cannot control is the weather. At the beginning of the week a storm had swept the English Channel, and it continued to batter the coasts of England and France.

These conditions seriously concerned Allied strategists, particularly the Supreme Commander, General Dwight D. Eisenhower. One of the six meteorologists who were advising Eisenhower at this critical time was a New Zealander, Lawrence Hogben, an instructor lieutenant-commander with the Royal New Zealand Navy. It was up to him and his colleagues to advise whether it was safe for D-Day to go ahead on 5 June. At their urging Eisenhower postponed the invasion,

American troops crowd the deck of a landing craft setting out for Normandy on D-Day. IMPERIAL WAR MUSEUM, EN 26341

leaving thousands of troops, seamen and aircrews on standby. The following day, in the most vital weather forecast of their lives, the team judged that a lull in the storm would last long enough for the landings to be completed safely. On their advice, Eisenhower decided that D-Day would be 6 June.

For those with direct responsibility for young lives there was apprehension about the conditions – Lieutenant Eric Krull thought it was 'borderline' whether they could make it to France and land the troops safely. Beach landings in Normandy were to begin from 6.30 in the morning, and so the thousands of ships left their harbours in southern England the night before. By that time thousands of troops had been crammed into their small landing craft for a day and a night, already buffeted by the storm. As the armada gathered at an assembly point in the Channel nicknamed Piccadilly Circus, the sea was still very rough. Seasickness was rife and, as they bucked their way to France, troops had to endure stench and squalor along with their fear of what lay ahead.

While parts of the Channel were churned white by the thousands of ships, the air above it was never busier than on D-Day. More than 3500 gliders and 1300 transport planes with their cargos of paratroops flew ahead of the fleet. Supporting the armada as it made the crossing were 7500 planes from the RAF and US Air Force. The night before, Bomber Command had flown more than 1200 sorties, its greatest total yet in one night. As well as continuing their attacks on railways and roads, crews had concentrated on enemy troop and gun positions, and bombed French ports where E-boats lay in wait for Allied ships.

As D-Day dawned, the superiority of the Allied air force was marked – in the 24 hours of 6 June they flew 14,000 sorties while the Luftwaffe managed less than 100. For the first time, George Wirepa's bomber squadron flew two raids in the space of twelve hours, one on some German artillery and the other on a bridge. Both raids successfully destroyed their targets. Fighter planes covered the landing beaches and fought off the odd German fighter that appeared. As Russell Clarke patrolled the coast, another Spitfire from his 485 (NZ) Squadron was the first that day to shoot down a German aircraft.

The brains behind the D-Day landings belonged to senior military leaders, but the action itself fell to young men, most in their late teens and early twenties. At 23, Lieutenant Jack Ingham, responsible for landing 200 troops, reflected on this as he stood on the bridge of his landing craft with the French coast in sight: 'It idly crossed my mind that there was a heck of lot of responsibility put into a lot of young heads. . . . The hard work was being done by people of my age, and there were thousands, all on the same business.' He felt 'very comfortable with the fact that we were managing it and doing it so well.'

British troops in a landing craft approaching Sword Beach, Normandy, on D-Day *(above)* and *(below)* struggling ashore, some helping the wounded. IMPERIAL WAR MUSEUM, B 5102 AND B 5114

The price of success

What lay ahead was a day of mixed fortunes, but for thousands of the young men, chaos and bloodshed awaited on the five landing beaches. Highest casualties were on Omaha in the American sector. It was on this most heavily defended of the D-Day beaches that Ned Hitchcock waded ashore under fire to find himself almost alone among dead bodies and burnt-out vehicles. More than 2000 men were killed, wounded or captured on this stretch of French coast. At Juno Beach, where Jack Ingham watched his precious cargo of troops make it to dry land, there were 1000 casualties, nearly all Canadians. On Gold Beach the same number of troops became casualties as Eric Krull endured the horrors of landing tanks under fire. The total number of Allied troops killed, injured or missing on D-Day was estimated at 10,000, less than military planners had expected. Among these, the dead numbered 2500. The number of German casualties is thought to have been between 4000 and 9000 men.

By the end of D-Day more than 130,000 men had been landed in Normandy. Operation Neptune was considered a success. At nightfall on 6 June, however, the Battle for Normandy had just begun. As the bomber pilot John Morris observed about the following weeks, 'Everybody began to realise things were not going as well as they should do. We were stuck there for a long time.' It would be another eleven months before the war in Europe was won.

Bombs away

One of the first objectives of Allied troops on D-Day was the city of Caen, a few kilometres inland from Sword Beach. It lay on a vital road and rail junction, and General Montgomery's plan was to take the city immediately, then drive along the short direct route to Paris. This plan was not to be realised. On D-Day, the city was a target of the battleship HMS *Ramillies*, and Jim Pollok, a lieutenant in its crew, is reflective as he recalls the sustained bombardment. 'If you're not particularly warlike, you realise you've wreaked an awful lot of destruction.' A great deal worse was to come before Caen fell to the Allies. When a month after D-Day the city was still in German hands, Montgomery requested a massive aerial strike. Late on 7 July, 447 planes from Bomber Command attacked. More than 5000 citizens of the devastated city died as a result. Within two days Allied troops finally captured Caen. The deaths there brought to 17,000 the total of French civilians killed in the war to that time. On the continent of Europe, they were not alone. From the beginning of 1942 Bomber Command had adopted a policy of deliberately bombing the most densely populated areas of German cities. What had begun the year before as retaliation for the Blitz became a deliberate and

A British soldier helps an elderly resident of Caen, Normandy, after Allied bombing devastated the town. July 1944. IMPERIAL WAR MUSEUM, B 6794

controversial strategy to break the morale of the German people and cause widespread dislocation. Often, several hundred planes would fly together to saturate one city with their bombs.

In the months after D-Day this Allied bombing of Germany intensified. While strategic military targets were still in Bomber Command's sights, the bombing of cities continued, and, as in the German bombing of British cities, incendiary bombs were widely used, causing firestorms in places such as Dresden, where an estimated 50,000 people were killed as a result. For the airmen involved in this bombing, the risks were high. As a bomb aimer, George Wirepa flew in many raids on Germany through this period, including one on Dresden. He reflects today on what he describes as 'a cruel war', and recalls feeling serious doubts, even at the time, about the need for such tactics. At the same time, he speaks for thousands of airmen who flew the raids when he describes the dangerous and vulnerable position of the aircrews themselves – more than 55,000 airmen from Bomber Command, nearly 1700 of them New Zealanders, were killed during the Second World War. George is blunt about his crew's determination to survive, even if it meant bombing away from their designated target: 'my main aim was to drop the bombs, get out and get back to base.'

The ruins of Dresden following Allied bombing raids that created firestorms, February 1945. IMPERIAL WAR MUSEUM, HU 3321

Among the thousands of airmen who went missing through this period, many became prisoners of war. New Zealanders Trevor Mullinder and John Morris were among those shot down over enemy territory after D-Day, to be captured, interrogated and imprisoned by the Germans. The first time John Morris bailed out of a burning plane he was helped to safety by members of the French Resistance, who constantly risked their lives to help Allied airmen. In this book we meet Lucienne Vouzelaud as she remembers, at the age of 93, her work in the Resistance and her association with the young John Morris. Her recollections, along with those of John and Trevor, offer insights into life and conditions in France and Germany in the last months of the war in Europe.

As Allied planes continued bombing Germany, a new terror was unleashed on the United Kingdom. A week after D-Day Germany began attacking London with V1 flying bombs, nicknamed 'doodlebugs'. Three months later the V2 rocket followed, continuing for six months in what became known as the Second Blitz. The V-weapons killed more than 8000 British civilians and injured many thousands more. Philip Stewart was one of the many skilled fighter pilots who successfully intercepted V1 flying bombs in the air, under instructions to destroy them before they reached London. The V2s, however, were unstoppable, and Philip recalls their

V1 flying bomb damage in London, 1944. This man returned from a Sunday morning walk to find his wife killed and his home destroyed. IMPERIAL WAR MUSEUM, D 21210

impact: 'The civilians, I think, were becoming desperately tired. The V1s had had an enormous effect, and then there were the V2s, which were even more terrifying and which nothing could be done about, and that had a big effect on morale.'

It was eleven months, almost to the day, after 'the big show' that the years of destruction and slaughter in Europe came to an end. Germany surrendered unconditionally to the Allies, and on 8 May 1945, Victory in Europe (VE) Day was celebrated. When peace came to Europe it settled on people who had seen unimaginable devastation and experienced abundant grief. In the years since September 1939, more than 60,000 civilians had been killed in the United Kingdom. In Germany civilian deaths numbered more than half a million. In the Battle of Normandy alone, from D-Day until the end of August 1944, more than 425,000 Allied and German troops were killed, wounded or went missing.

Being there

War on this scale is difficult to comprehend, and the history of such a war can lose meaning when it is reduced to a collection of significant dates, major actions and casualty numbers. Oral history adds another dimension to understanding the experience and impact of war, particularly when it is gathered from people whose stories are not included in the official accounts. This is such a collection. It offers the perspective of a group of New Zealanders who travelled to the other side of the world to be part of one of the most defining periods in history.

The memories and reflections of the men in this book reveal some common ground. Notably, each approached the war with a willingness to serve. At the beginning of the following century, it is hard to imagine thousands of young men from a Pacific country signing up for armed service in a war being fought in Europe. But the late 1930s and 1940s were very different years, culturally, socially and politically. Then, allegiance to Great Britain, the King, the Empire and all it represented dominated New Zealand society. Many Pakeha New Zealanders still called the United Kingdom 'home'. The generation represented in this book reflects this. It saw its place in the world in a way those in their late teens and early twenties today may find hard to imagine. Government propaganda and social pressure played their part in encouraging conformity, but, apart from a relatively small group of conscientious objectors, the majority of young men did not question the need to join up. Some enlisted because they were seeking adventure, others wanted to stick with their mates. Many genuinely wanted to stop Hitler, and the attitude of bomber pilot Les Munro sums up their motivation for service: 'We had a job to do, come what may.'

The men in this book also shared an impatience to get on with the long-awaited invasion of France. Like all Allied servicemen and -women, and civilians, they looked forward to D-Day as the beginning of the end of the war in Europe. When it finally happened, everyone who witnessed aspects of the invasion recalls feeling a sense of awe at the sheer scale of the endeavour. They came home with indelible memories of the sight of the armada churning across the Channel, the sky above it dark with planes, the French coast smoky through the dawn. They shared in the exhilaration when they learnt the invasion had been successful.

Some Second World War veterans have a tendency to understate experience, perhaps a reflection of Kiwi male culture among their generation. But a lack of flourish does not necessarily mean an absence of emotion. There are things that are lost when oral history is transcribed to the page – the faltering voice, the pause to gather composure, the silence that accompanies memories too painful to express. In these pages, acts of courage, feats of endurance, memories of horror, experiences of fear and grief are described simply, without drama.

Until now we have not recognised, collectively, the 10,000 New Zealanders who were serving in Europe at the time of Operation Overlord and Operation Neptune. The men in this book convey something of the energy and spirit of those operations, as well as the impact of the losses and weariness that come with years at war. Some concede disillusionment that their efforts of more than 60 years ago, costing so much in terms of human life, have not created a better world. As Philip Stewart puts it, 'sadness that it was not the war to end all wars, that there is no such thing.'

It would be wrong to overstate the similarities between these men. They are individuals from diverse backgrounds, with different personalities and different perspectives on the epic years they were part of. Their stories speak for themselves. Together, they represent those from a generation of New Zealanders who found themselves at war in Europe. As decorated fighter pilot Russell Clarke says, 'We were just the ordinary boys in the street in those days . . . . any cross-section in the street, they'd have done the same. . . . Just time and place determined that we were the ones that were doing it.'

Jack Ingham, 1943. JACK INGHAM COLLECTION

Jack Ingham DSC

LIEUTENANT, LCI(L) 302 AND LCI(L) 110, RN

Getting these guys on the beach, that was all that mattered.

PETONE BEACH WAS JACK INGHAM'S CHILDHOOD PLAYGROUND. BORN IN THE SMALL settlement on Wellington Harbour in 1920, he loved the sea and at the age of eleven joined the Sea Scouts. When war was declared he wrote to the Royal New Zealand Navy and along with ten other young Post Office telegraphists was 'loaned' to the Royal Navy, who had sought their skills. Jack had a sense of duty and was committed to the cause, saying of Hitler, 'The only way to stop bullies is to bounce them.'

Two months before his twentieth birthday, in October 1940, he sailed from Wellington for England on the *Rangitata*. As the ship docked in Liverpool the reality of the war in Europe hit him.

> I was scared stiff. I think we all were. We got a feeling that we'd come to the war when we sailed up the Mersey River. They'd had raids the night before and the houses on the riverside, they were still burning. The smell of burnt sugar always reminds me of that, the warehouse of Tate and Lyle, the big sugar conglomerate that got hit and the smell was like toffee, making toffee. We were in the war. And that night we were allowed three or four hours ashore in Liverpool and there was an air raid – we went to a troop concert, and coming out there was an air raid and the locals saw that we were wandering about and showed us where a shelter was. You'd see the tracer going up, the shells bursting in the air from our guns and otherwise the whole place being blacked out. All you

could see was buildings burning if they'd been hit. I never got used to air raids, but you suffered them.

On leave in London during the Blitz, Jack became more familiar with the experience of being bombed. Evidence of destruction was everywhere.

> Some nights, if we were caught away, we spent the night in the subway in the Underground, and to come out and find the amount of wreckage that had been done during the night was pretty scary. Picking your way through loads of bricks to find your way back to your billets. The bombs are terrifying things and the Undergrounds were the common refuge for most people. They were crowded. People were just lying with their mattresses and their blankets and so on. But they were a jolly lot, the Cockneys, and they didn't mind you getting down and sharing their rug or their blanket or something like that . . . children crying at night, and the trains constantly coming down, but you learned to sleep through it.

What about if you were out on the street?

> Well, you'd take shelter in a doorway. The danger was, besides the bombs falling, the amount of shrapnel from our own guns that was coming down, and so it was sensible to get into a doorway. It was a bit spooky because you'd hear shrapnel going bim bang all the way down, hitting the ground. And if a bomb lands fairly close, well it's like an earthquake,

Bomb damage following an air raid on Liverpool, England, c. 1942. IMPERIAL WAR MUSEUM, D 5983

Jack Ingham and a friend, Paul McGee, on leave in Trafalgar Square, London, April 1941.
JACK INGHAM COLLECTION

the whole ground shakes and the big, big bang after the explosion. If you see the explosion, then a big bang comes a few seconds afterwards and you get the air rushing at you. So that was a blitz. But the Cockney people – they never had a clue how they were going to win the war, they were taking such a battering, but you couldn't convince them that they would ever lose it. Great spirit. We came across [to England] as cynical colonials, and being part of the scene in London changed your mind. You started to admire them, the fact that they weren't going to give in, weren't going to be beaten. It changed your whole attitude towards them. It did me anyway.

London was a magnet. I think it's because you felt you were part of history and every possible occasion we'd be in London. The New Zealand Forces Club was sort of a meeting place, and you were bound to meet somebody that you knew either in the air force or the navy. And of course the Second Echelon of the New Zealand Division, they were sent to UK rather than the Middle East to help, as part of the anti-invasion force. The New Zealand Forces Club was a popular place for any of the services. It was a good place – they had showers for people that needed showering, liquor and good meals.

Any rivalry between the different services?

Oh a lot of leg-pulling, of course. Yes, the glamour boys of the air force were good for a leg-pull. And the army were gradually being sent to the Middle East, but I always met a few army people that I knew, schoolmates, Petone people.

Other favourite spots for a night out in London were the Lyons Corner Houses, a chain of restaurants that provided reasonably priced food.

It was such an entertaining evening for so little – a cup of coffee, a cup of tea. And the big ones all had orchestras or bands and you could just sit and listen, and I had a favourite one and the leading violinist used to wander around playing to groups at the tables, and he spotted the New Zealand tabs on me and asked if I had a popular song I wanted. But he didn't know 'Pokarekare Ana' – he played 'Waltzing Matilda' and got in with the Aussies.

Keeping their spirits up. Jack Ingham, second from left, enjoys a Sunday-morning drink with friends at a country pub, March 1941. JACK INGHAM COLLECTION

For some months after their arrival in England, Jack and his mates were in training, based at Chatham Barracks on the Kent coast. Conditions there were tough.

> They were terrible. Tremendously crowded for a start, and because it was south coast and a naval base, it was expecting to be bombed and it got bombed regularly. Practically every day planes were over to drop a few on the naval base and hope to hit something, and any that didn't hit the naval base quite often hit the living quarters. So air raids, you took to tunnels. Chatham being on the side of a hill, they tunnelled in and made the air-raid shelters in the tunnels, and everybody had to go there at night if they weren't on duty, fire-watching or manning guns or sentry duty – otherwise you were in the tunnel. And they were still getting their air conditioning working as fast as they could, but with the crowds and crowds that were down there slinging hammocks or sleeping on the floor, the air was all thick. When you came out in the morning and hit the fresh air it was like running into a brick wall. Terrible. And coughing and snivelling.

> *Did you feel any fear through that period?*

> If you were caught outside, but you got a bit nonchalant about it, a bit blasé, because it was happening so often. You got the feeling, yeah, if your number's up you cop it.

It was in Chatham Barracks that Jack first heard Winston Churchill's rousing speeches on the radio, and he remembers them vividly.

> Chatham Barracks had about 12,000 people in it, and that was more than the population of Petone. And when it was time for his speech the whole barracks went silent, and if you dared speak while you were waiting, somebody would tell you to shut up, and it was just magic listening. At the end of it everybody clapped and cheered and carried on. You got the feeling that if he could feel like that, why can't we?

Along with two other New Zealanders, Jack was drafted to HMS *Royal Ulsterman* as a radio operator in July 1941. The ship was a Combined Operations troop trainer and troop carrier, and in his first three months on board it travelled to Iceland and Scotland before transporting troops to the African coast. A year after he left home, Jack was on the *Royal Ulsterman* in dock at Clyde when a troopship arrived.

It had just come in and was disembarking passengers. It had anchored off – it hadn't come in alongside and they had a tender, a small tugboat sort of thing that loaded up and dropped them in and then went back for another load, and this particular one that was coming in, there was a crowd of New Zealanders on and they started singing 'Now is the Hour'. I was very, very homesick at that stage. They were just servicemen disembarking and, yes, greatly excited to hear this, and so I waited by the dockside until they landed and had a good Kiwi talk.

Along with his three New Zealand friends Jack was accepted for training for a commission in the middle of 1942. In December he passed out of Naval College in Brighton as a sub-lieutenant with Combined Operations, attached to the 'raiding force'. Landing craft were being built for the job in England. Others were being built in the United States, and their reputation among British sailors was glowing.

Knowing the Americans' love of luxury, the stories were that these American-built landing craft were something that you had to get. The British ones were just spartan. They were the minimum of everything, most uncomfortable. So when we got drafted to America there was jubilation. The Americans love luxury, and these were quite comfortable LCIs. LCI(L) is the proper title. Landing Craft Infantry, Large because there were two sorts, the smaller kind too.

Jack was sent to New York to pick up one of the many landing craft being built for the British navy. When he arrived in America the contrast with wartime England was stark.

Amazing. Got there on the Sunday night and went out on the town with everything blazing and lights going, clubs going, and wandered around until midnight and decided that it hadn't been overemphasised, that the Yanks had every right to talk big, because after the blackout and the lack of glamour in UK, the bright lights of New York were just too much.

When, after three weeks on one landing craft as first lieutenant, Jack was drafted to another as commanding officer, he felt the sudden responsibility. By this time he had considerable experience at sea, but handling a crew of 25 men was more daunting. He took command of LCI(L) 302 in April 1943. His first lieutenant was Keith Williamson from Dunedin, with whom he had travelled to America.

We saw as much of New York as we could, but when the 302 was finished we were busy for the next week, getting a little bit of experience in handling them. But to begin with, the first two days a pilot was needed to help us through the teething troubles of learning how to drive the damned thing. The crew were mostly kids straight out from barracks – eighteen, nineteen, twenty. The oldest was the coxswain, he was 28 and he'd been a London bobby.

When the ship was ready I stood by for a couple of days while they were putting the finishing touches to it. These darn things were prefabricated all over the country, little industries were given the job of making perhaps a hatch or another piece and then put on trains and sent to the dockside and stitched together by women welders, and gradually the ship took shape. And so when it was finally finished they just pushed it into the sea. No ceremony.

The living conditions were lovely – a shared cabin and a small shower room with a handbasin and a toilet in it. Beautiful, beautiful American bits and pieces. We had a big ice chest and a refrigerator and a coffee-making machine, and all things went by electricity. That was good unless the electricity failed, as it sometimes did through inexperience of the electrician, otherwise they were beautifully comfortable. The officers' cabin, for instance, we had bunks. Very comfortable – reading lamps and things. And then the crew had their own living space down below. There were three big, big troop compartments to house the 250 troops, and ships were fitted with eight big bus engines. You see anything that was available was used for anything that was going to be fairly short-lived. The expectation was that these landing ships . . . the losses were going to be pretty heavy, so they didn't want to spend too much money on them. Bus engines were available, so there were eight bus engines, four on each propeller. That made them fairly powerful, could get up to 15–16 knots, 20 knots if you wanted to blow the thing apart.

Jack's ship joined a fleet of twenty ships to cross the Atlantic, heading for the Mediterranean to train in beaching techniques with the 51st Highland Division of the Eighth Army on the North African coast. In Sicily the crew had their first experience of landing under fire from land and air.

I was scared to start off with, but then you got so busy you forgot about it. After the initial shock of finding that being fired at was unhappy and unhealthy but we were still surviving, you just hoped for the best. There was quite a lot of fire from the land until the troops got established, but after that it was only air. They were constantly overhead for the first three or four weeks.

As commanding officer, Jack was in a vulnerable position standing on the bridge of his landing craft, but he was becoming increasingly confident in his new role.

> If you're busy, your brain is on what you're supposed to be doing, at least that is what I found. When you were busy, your thoughts were getting there safely, getting back safely, the dangers of beaching and not being able to get off a beach. And there were all those technical things to occupy your mind. All the time we were doing this we were gaining a tremendous amount of experience and in fact we were the experts of this new type of craft. We were the experts handling these damn things, and all these kids, like myself, getting a bit big-headed about it. But we were getting good experience in all sorts of conditions.

In early December Jack left the Mediterranean and headed back to England, where he was assigned to another landing craft and further training in beach landings. Preparation for D-Day was intensifying. In May 1944 Jack moved to LCI(L) 110, another landing craft for infantry. He was reluctant to leave a crew he had grown close to and hoped the new posting would be to a good ship. But a challenge lay ahead – Commander Alan Villiers assigned Jack to this post because he believed he could turn the crew around.

> The ship I was sent to, 110, had been a sort of black sheep in the flotilla, some way or other it had never been on any operations, had suffered a lot of breakdowns, spent a lot of time alongside being repaired . . . and Villiers had this in his care and was reluctant to take it on, but he had to. And so he told me, 'The bloody thing hasn't earned its keep, Jack, and you're expected to get it working.' This was just a few weeks before D-Day.

> *You weren't to know exactly how close D-Day was, were you?*

> No, but the feeling was that it wasn't going to be long. And so I was very sourpuss taking over, and the crew were sourpuss as well.

Jack's first lieutenant was another very young man, Adrian Liddle, known as Tiddly. The landing craft they were on was one of the early ones and its crew were older and more experienced.

Jack Ingham uses the sextant on his landing craft, June 1944.

They'd been on LCIs for a long time, knew their seamanship, knew their way around, absolutely grumpy because they'd been the laughing-stock of the flotilla, you see. The feeling was that nobody likes us and we don't like ourselves, and they were grumpy and I was grumpy. All they wanted to do was to get the war over. And so I had to treat them very officially, play by the book – no friendships – and I was the 'Colonial Bastard'. That was my nickname – behind my back, but I knew it.

How did you turn that around?

Working them, work hard, and they could see that I knew as much about LCIs as they did. And they couldn't put anything across me there. Once we got to work everybody realised that it was better to do the work and get it over and done with. We got through it and we joined the flotilla after we'd put in a week or so in London, and the flotilla were further down the river using the banks of the river for beaching practice. The tide sweeping up and sweeping down was a good training ground as it turned out, because Normandy had the strong tide running up and down.

The crew had the experience of these ships, they'd been there from the beginning of them and all that was needed was just enthusiasm. I saw them losing their surliness and their attitude, the way they moved around instead of sleeping and stooping around. They started holding their heads up and moving a bit faster. I had a good wardroom steward, he was a telltale really. He used to bring me tales from the lower deck and he told me one day, 'Oh sir, you're not the Colonial Bastard downstairs any more,' he says, 'you're Jacko', and so that was a victory. I started looking at them differently then.

What was the mood in those days immediately before D-Day?

Sort of revenge, in a mild way. I thought so, yes. Now it's your turn, son. And after seeing places like Plymouth and Coventry and have the insides of a city busted flat you could sympathise. Pretty cold-hearted way to look at it, but yes, returns.

Three days before D-Day the LCI crews were briefed on their role and the overall plans for the landings, including details of the air support. LCI(L) 110 was to transport 200 men of the 51st Highland Division across the English Channel and land them on Juno Beach to join troops from a Canadian division.

The size of the operation was awe-inspiring, and you couldn't see how it could be anything else but victory. Our turn for victory was getting the troops on the beach and getting them supplied. What happened after that was up to the army. There was nothing gung-ho about it, they were just there to do a job. The 51st had a reputation of being a first-class regiment and they were just there to get it over and done with. They were a very veteran infantry group. There was no glamour as far as they were concerned and no John Wayne stuff – let's get the job over and done with and get back home.

When D-Day was delayed because of bad weather, a signal was sent to all the landing craft commanding officers advising them, if possible, to hold a church service before departure.

That's when the storm got worse. We held the church service, and it was pretty nerve-wracking if you're not a padre. You've got a little handbook –

the Admiralty think of everything – a handbook, *Conduct of Church Services in His Majesty's Service*. So I just followed that, and the weather in itself was pretty awesome. A small ship at anchor in a storm, everything's making a noise – the creaks of the ship, the rain belting into you and the flags flapping away up there, the wind howling through the aerials, it's pretty noisy. All the soldiers, if they wanted to, could attend, and quite a lot of the army stood around joining in. Nerve-wracking. Oh dear, it was quite an eerie experience, and as I heard one guy saying, 'Whose side do you think He's on, sending us this storm?'

At one point in the service, Jack had to read from Psalm 107, the 'Sailors' Psalm' – 'for at His word the stormy wind ariseth which lifteth up the waters thereof'.

Spooky, yeah. And we sang just the first verse of 'Eternal Father, Strong To Save'.

How did the troops respond to the news of the postponement?

Oh, phlegmatic – another one of those brass-hat decisions, they don't know what they're talking about, that sort of attitude. The crew fussed around them like old hens and they supported them when they could, gave them the free run of the ship. They had their special turns at the galley and the toilets and all that, shared very well. I was getting to change my attitude towards the crew as well. I saw they were human. They'd found out by that time that they were as good as any other ship in the squadron at the business we were at, so their morale was good.

The 24 hours we were waiting, the army had to keep spruced up of course, army discipline, and they had to keep shaven and clean and tidy and everything else. They brought these special rations that had to last them for some time, and among them were these tins of soup and inside the tin was another tube with a little wick on the top, and when you lit this wick it sort of burned down and it heated up the soup. Now that was fine and dandy but these boys were quick on the job, they emptied the soup out, filled it up with water, lit the tube and they had hot water to shave!

The soldiers were seasick, tossing round at the end of an anchor. The ship's on the move always, constantly, yawing, bucking up and down, and there were a lot seasick. Conditions were crowded – each troop deck housed about 50 and had its own little toilet. But they were pretty smelly by the time there were a few seasick guys. They were on there two days by the time they got off, although the army officers, that was their job to attend to the morale of their guys. They did what they could in keeping them clean. We supplied the buckets and mops and things. The storm was the fault, because the boys had been to sea often enough, the sailors, and the soldiers, certainly they'd had their share of ships and seasickness.

Did that have any effect on their morale? It would have left them feeling physically a bit under the weather.

I don't think it did, no. They realised they had a seat across, and at the end of the crossing they could get their business over and done with.

We were told by signal to be prepared to leave some time during the morning or early afternoon, and after lunch the flag hoist went up, Sail – and up anchor and off we go. It got your belly a little bit, because it was bad enough in the Thames Estuary, that was getting a battering, but once we got outside into the straits, then you got the full force of the wind and it was dying down gradually, but it was still pretty powerful. Very rough conditions. And so we all lined up in formation and got out into the Channel and off we go round past the straits, the Seven Sisters, the Straits of Dover.

I was just amazed at the number of ships that could be crowded into a small ocean. They came from everywhere. They were in front of us, tailing us. . . . And we all had times to reach certain points, because other parts of the invasion had to mesh in. And off Portsmouth there was this junction where three convoys had to merge together to get along a narrow swept channel. The English Channel was laden with minefields and you had to be in swept channels to be sure of not getting blown up, and so there was this narrow swept channel that the minesweepers had been sweeping for days and nights across to the beaches. And by this time it was getting night, and as dark was falling we had to mesh with some big LSTs coming in from Portsmouth and they were going to be inside us, we were going to be tucked away on their outside, and with the weather conditions and the darkness coming, that was quite a feat getting into position, but everybody managed it.

One interesting thing happened there. I decided to leave the bridge for a while and get a cup of coffee or something, and I got down to the cabin and a messenger came down to say that the first lieutenant wanted me. And he said, 'I'm sorry but I can't see, I'm night-blind.' And I thought for a while and then the penny dropped – we'd never done a night exercise. He'd

British commandos on board a landing craft bound for Sword Beach, Normandy, on D-Day.
IMPERIAL WAR MUSEUM, BU 1181

come straight from naval college with no conception of the difference in night-time. And I said, 'Have you ever done any night work?', and he said, 'Never.' So OK, I stayed on the bridge for half an hour, three-quarters of an hour, and just gave him a general difference, that you can tell the distance between the ship ahead if you read the signs of his wake. If it's nice and big and bubbly, you're too damned close. After three-quarters of an hour, he got confident. But I thought then, with those sophisticated and involved plans, pages upon pages upon pages that we'd been reading about the planning that had gone into this operation, and that vital little thing was missing. Somebody had overlooked the fact that this was going to take place at night, we'd better do some night practice. Made you giggle, really.

It took the landing craft three to four hours to cross the Channel.

The wind was easing, the seas weren't quite as bad, and about midnight came the drone overhead, hundreds and hundreds of planes going across. This was the bombers first, they were going to do what damage they could on the beaches. And then the clouds parted every now and again and you could see the shapes going over, hundreds and hundreds of planes. Then there was a lull, and then another batch of planes came across, and they made a different noise from the bombers and these were the Dakotas towing the gliders and the parachutists. We knew we were getting close to France by that time. The messenger on board, he looked up and said, 'I'm glad I'm not one of those guys.' Didn't fancy their job.

Keeping station was pretty difficult because of the weather conditions, keeping in your right place in the line of ships and those of you abreast of each other. I went down a couple of times and had a cup of coffee, but with Tiddly being so young and inexperienced I wouldn't have slept anyway, so I spent most of the time on the bridge.

As dawn was breaking, each second that it got lighter there'd be more ships you could see further out, just an amazing sight. Ships of all shapes and sizes, and very comforting to see the big battleships there. The sea was thick with them. It idly crossed my mind that there was a heck of lot of responsibility put into a lot of young heads. I'm sure that's the usual thing in war, isn't it? It's the young ones that do the business and the older ones that direct the business. But the hard work was being done by people of my age, and there were thousands, all on the same business. They could have been bankers, they could have been post office employees, could have been gardeners. And yes, I felt, not exactly arrogant, but very comfortable with the fact that we were managing it and doing it so well.

At dawn we were about fifteen miles off Juno Beach. This was quite different from what we'd been used to. The other invasions had usually taken place at dawn to get the element of surprise that is most critical, and as far as possible at high tide, so that when you landed the troops they only had a small amount of space to get out from the boat over sand and into action. But this time they reversed things, and because of the number of beach obstacles that had to be demolished to get anywhere near the beach itself, they decided to wait for low tide and daylight so the frogmen could have a reasonable chance of destroying the beach obstacles.

Frogmen had been landed from small assault craft to destroy the obstacles and defuse the mines attached to many of them. As Jack's ship approached Juno Beach the noise of battle was almost overpowering.

Endless gunfire from ships, the warships, from the cruisers, from the destroyers, and they were all belting hell out of enemy artillery positions trying to silence them. And the storm itself was pretty noisy, of course, but no it was the gunfire. You had to shout at all to make yourself heard. Every time you shouted a command down the voice-pipe they had to repeat it back to you to make sure they heard it properly.

The first wave went in at low tide, ahead of us, and as a matter of fact as we got nearer a lot of those craft were coming back, returning. And our job – we were going in at half tide, and our 51st were hoping to land on beaches that were in our possession, or fairly secure. That was nearly the case, not quite. The wind was still roaring, still very fierce. The sea was up, and it made manoeuvring pretty difficult. So it was time for ours to land, the beaches were getting pretty littered with wreckage. Landing craft that had been mined and holed and landing craft that had been shot up on a beach and that sort of stuff. And getting closer, there were plenty of bodies floating around too. Didn't let your mind dwell on that because you could have been the next one. Getting these guys on the beach, that was all that mattered. And this is where training came into it, really. You had all the techniques of doing so, but you had to be careful that you used them and you didn't get sloppy or haphazard about it because you'd be the next wreckage. So the CO of the troops, he was on the bridge with me and getting very interested as we got closer, and of course when you got close enough he was down with his troops there, getting them ready to get off. Being a good keen Scotsman he had a little hip flask in his pocket and we had nips of that, whisky.

We realised why we'd been training in those sort of conditions. The tide is sweeping you downwards and so you have to go in like a crab, pointing 'up there' and hoping to get 'down there'. All our practice had been beautifully done like a military parade ground. They'd gone in one, two, three together, beached, drawn off. The next three together, drawn off – all very good, you see, because there was no opposition and no strong winds. And when we got close enough, Commander Villiers recognised this wasn't going to happen, so he just ordered, 'Beach independently'. And so it was up to each one of us to find a gap that we thought was suitable and get cracking.

It was up to yourself then. I saw a fellow officer going in and I was behind him. And he had one go and it wasn't suitable, he'd hit a sandbank first, so he cleared off and I came in alongside him and got on the same sandbank. Water was too deep to get the troops off, so we kedged off and tried another way. But then you had to be careful that further down there might have been some wreckage and some more beach obstacles. But I went in again, had got quite close, got pretty good on the beach, got over the sandbank OK, and that wasn't a worry, because getting over the sandbank full with troops meant that coming off I'd be floating lighter, so that wasn't a worry, and we got in much better the second time, and sent two boys over on each ramp to test the depth of the water. It was up to their waist, and so I told the CO troops that might be the best I could manage and was he prepared to get off in that depth? And so off they went.

It was a gut-wrenching moment to see them going off. When you beach you ride up onto the surf, onto the beach or as close as you can, and then these two ramps are lowered. It's a steep run down to the beach and then, when the troops are all off, you pull the ramps up.

Jack vividly remembers watching as the 200 troops ran down the ramps, loaded with gear.

Heavily, heavily laden and that's why, had they been in water much deeper, with the wave action they would have been swept off their feet and no chance of getting up once they were down. But they did, all except six. The wind had driven me off by then and I would have had to have made another beaching to get these six off, and that was a bit of a worry because we'd been told to get the ship back unscathed as far as possible, to get the next load across the Channel. There was one of the smaller craft, just coming off empty, so we hailed him and said, 'Can you take six ashore for me?' He said, 'Yeah, pop them over', so they got ashore.

And were you aware of watching all of them?

Yes. Yes. Before they went, the CO came up and shook hands.

What did he say?

'Thanks for the ride'.

There was still a fair bit of activity, light arms fire coming from the shore and howitzers that hadn't been silenced. There was a fair bit of fireworks still as well as the congestion on the beach. The beach looked like a wrecker's yard. But strangely enough none of the fellows got hit aboard, although there was plenty of rattling going on, small arms fire hitting the boat. Quite a number of landing craft had gone down. Some of them were on the beach burning, and some that had sunk were in the water. And there were plenty of bodies floating about.

British commandos scramble ashore from their landing craft on Juno Beach on D-Day.
IMPERIAL WAR MUSEUM, B 5218

When they got onto the sand, did any of the troops turn around?

Yeah. Waved, God bless us. I felt pretty satisfied, satisfied that I'd got them that far, and sorry as hell to see them go.

Jack heard later that the troops from his ship did well in France. He was awarded a Distinguished Service Cross for his actions on D-Day, but considers the award was for his ship, rather than for himself personally.

Between D-Day and November 1944, Jack's landing craft made between 30 and 40 trips across the Channel, taking more troops over and bringing back the wounded. On one occasion, soon after D-Day, they returned to England with German prisoners. In early December he and the crew of LCI(L) 110 took their ship to Scotland where, along with hundreds of others, it was to be scrapped.

It was rather moving, because we were taken up to Loch Fyne where I'd started all this Combined Operation business in the *Royal Ulsterman*, and there were trots and trots and trots of LCIs all laid up. And we'd had a vicious trip up, there'd been a pretty bad storm coming through the English Channel and up through the Irish Sea, and it was rather refreshing to get

Landing craft speed across the English Channel on one of the many return trips after D-Day, transporting reinforcements and bringing back wounded and German POWs.
JACK INGHAM COLLECTION

into this placid loch. It was wintertime of course, and we tied up at a buoy with five or six other LCIs and the crew were taken off and we all met in a motor bus ready to leave, and it had been snowing. When we got to the top of the hill going out from the loch we looked back and saw the hills encrusted with snow and these lines and lines of LCIs sitting there. One of the crew said, 'Oh, it wasn't a bad old bugger after all, was it?' Silence for a while, till they got chatting again on the bus. But they were all moved alright.

In March 1945, Jack returned home to New Zealand with his English wife, Jean Powell, whom he had met and married in Liverpool. The couple had three children. Jack became a schoolteacher and retired in 1979. Jean died in 2000 after 58 years of marriage. Jack later remarried and he and his wife, Betty Bryers-Ingham, live most of the time in Tauranga, where Jack commemorates Anzac Day.

Our meeting place is the war memorial almost down at the Mount on Ocean Beach, and Anzac Day there is a buzz because you're looking

Jack Ingham, 2004. ALISON PARR

straight out over the sea, and the dawn comes. They have a couple of aeroplanes that fly over and they've got this crowd that increases year by year, and as the dawn comes you look out to the water. You can remember all the dawns that you had at sea, when you're waiting for daybreak so that we can get below and change watches and get your head down and have a sleep. It all comes back. So Anzac Day is worth its time and its effort to get up for that dawn.

And sometimes on Anzac Day, Jack can see in his mind the French coast on D-Day.

That, again, brings a sense of pride. That dawn when you got surrounded by ships, and as it got lighter and lighter you could see more ships and more ships behind you, and ahead of you, and the French coast was covered in smoke, but you knew it was there.

Philip Stewart, 1942. PHILIP STEWART COLLECTION

Philip Stewart MID

FLIGHT LIEUTENANT, NO. 1, 129 AND 616 SQUADRONS,
FIGHTER COMMAND, RAF

*One was part of something which involved many thousands of
people and an enormous amount of planning. If it failed it would
be a complete disaster, so it had to succeed.*

BEFORE THE WAR PHILIP STEWART WAS SO INTRIGUED BY FLYING THAT HE PAID TEN
shillings for a circuit over Wanganui in a Tiger Moth. His first taste of low-level
flying came when the pilot 'beat up' the tennis court where friends were playing.

Philip was born in Wanganui in 1917 and hoped to be a doctor, but the
Depression put paid to that ambition. His father's business went bankrupt and
Philip had to leave school without matriculating. He needed to earn money, and
his first job was as a wool clerk. His family thought of the United Kingdom as
'home', and when war was declared a sense of patriotism convinced Philip to join
up. It was not only his attraction to flying that drew him to the air force.

> I had a horror of any form of warfare which was mainly thrusting bayonets
> through people, in other words hand-to-hand combat of the sort that we
> heard so much about in the First World War. I thought, well, at least in the
> navy or the air force it would be much more impersonal. You were unlikely
> to see the person you might be shooting down or responsible for killing,
> and to my mind that appealed quite a bit. I think that was the most deciding
> factor.

Like many hundreds of other young men at the time, Philip's first flying lessons
were in Tiger Moths, on the Taieri Plains near Dunedin. He took easily to flying,
but tragedy marred his early experience. A fellow trainee pilot was killed on his
first solo flight when he failed to do a circuit of Taieri aerodrome on landing and

A trainee pilot about to take off in a Tiger Moth at Taieri aerodrome, near Dunedin.
Hundreds of New Zealand wartime pilots had their first flying lessons in these planes.
AIR FORCE MUSEUM, CHRISTCHURCH, PR6344

crashed head-on into the Tiger Moth Philip was taking off in with his instructor.
The instructor was seriously injured. Philip was unharmed and flew again three
days later, but the short delay prevented him leaving for Canada with his group of
trainee pilots – a blow at the time. In spite of this, over the months that followed
Philip's love of flying grew, particularly in fighter planes.

> It's a sense of freedom, that's why I was delighted to go on the fighters and
> not on the bombers, because you were on your own, you could do what
> you liked more or less, go in any direction, a great sort of sense of freedom.
> I had a horror of being put on the bombers and being responsible for a
> number of other lives as a pilot, and I was very relieved indeed that I was a
> fighter instead.

In 1941 Philip left for Canada as one of the thousands of young New Zealanders
who polished their skills in the Empire Air Training Scheme. The early days of
training in Canada were marred by more losses. He recalls 'just acting as pall-bear-
ers for guys who were crashing around the aerodrome' while his group waited for
some weeks to be transferred for further training. In October 1941, after six months
in Canada, he left for Scotland to convert to Spitfires – and more lives were claimed.
Five out of his course of 30 were killed during that time.

Philip Stewart climbing into his Spitfire, Ibsley, Hampshire, 1943. PHILIP STEWART COLLECTION

At the end of the year Philip became part of 91 Squadron, and two months later he moved to 129 Squadron, in which he served until April 1943. He revelled in the power and manoeuvrability of Spitfires and was impatient to get into combat. As bomber escorts, 129 Squadron took part in the infamous Dieppe raid, in which the Canadians suffered heavy losses. 129 Squadron was often engaged in dogfights over England and the Channel, 'inviting' the Luftwaffe into battle. Each enemy aircraft confirmed to have been shot down was called a 'definite'. Those which were thought to have been shot down were called 'probables'. Because of the chaos of such fighting, the numbers were often unclear.

> I don't think I had any that I could claim as absolutely definites. I claimed
> a number of probables, but was never able to have absolute confirmation,
> I think mainly because when I did hit something things could become
> confusing, or I realised I was being shot at. You were very much engaged
> in shooting at one of the Luftwaffe aircraft. It might have been one of their
> bombers or it might have been another fighter. Whilst you were busy doing
> that, something else crept up on your tail and started firing at you. These

aerial battles – it was difficult to come back with any clear picture of what had happened or even exactly how many aircraft had attacked you or how many you were attacking.

Did you ever have any sense when you were firing at planes that there was another man, there were other men involved?

No. It was an aircraft. You didn't think about the guy flying it. You really didn't see them. If you were close enough you might see a helmet in the cockpit, but there was no sense of identity. No, it was an aircraft that you had to stop doing whatever it was about to do. So far as the fighter was concerned it was you or 'he', and the 'he' was impersonal. The 'he' was an aircraft.

How did you cope with the fact that your number could be up at any time?

I don't think you necessarily thought about it. You had a feeling that you, of all people, were probably very unlikely to ever be killed. I didn't think about it like that anyway. Very, very few did. On one or two occasions where pilots of my own flight suffered from what they called 'lack of moral fibre', all that happened to the poor beggars was that they became afraid. It got on top of them. Maybe they had been in battles where two or three of the squadron had been lost, good friends of theirs, and they suddenly, for all sorts of reasons, would turn back from a flying operation on the excuse that they had a problem with their cockpit hood or something was wrong with the aircraft. It was eventually discovered that they were just frightened, and you had to take them off flying. But the majority, I would say, didn't think of it that way – I'm impervious, I'll be alright.

Did you ever experience fear?

Yes, every time I got into the cockpit. You always had a sinking feeling in your stomach when you were going off on a sortie, worst of all if it was one which was arranged well and truly ahead. You had a briefing and knew exactly what we were going to do. Then there was a long wait where you sat in your aircraft waiting to take off. I think that never ceased to be, and I've spoken to other guys who had exactly the same feeling. It was, I suppose, a form of fear. We didn't know what was going to happen.

No idea. Sometimes everyone came back and it was almost boring, and other times it was extremely hectic. You just didn't know.

But when you were scrambled, when there was an emergency, that was another matter, because you just had to get into the aircraft as quickly as possible and take off as fast as you could, and that was that – you didn't have time to get the butterflies in your stomach.

Philip recalls that most of the squadron smoked heavily. Cigarettes, fast cars and alcohol were all part of the lifestyle.

We used to drink, yes. I can remember very hectic sessions in the messes – very often of course we were unable to leave aerodromes, and we would have terrific sessions in the mess and play all sorts of stupid games. Mind you, there wasn't much hard alcohol. There was very little whisky or anything like that available. It was mostly beer, and it was pretty weak beer at that.

Some of Philip's fellow airmen in 129 Squadron with his Alsatian, Jan, in 1943. The dog travelled to different bases with Philip and enjoyed chasing Spitfires when they were taking off. PHILIP STEWART COLLECTION

How much was the drinking part of coping with what you were living through?

I think that's probably quite a big bit. Because, well, it sounds a bit gruesome and unpleasant, but sometimes you'd come back and you would find that two or three of the squadron had not come back. It might turn out that one of those was a guy you were sharing a bedroom with and usually a reasonable mate, if not best mate. It just didn't pay to dwell on it too much, obviously, and so there was a bit of talk about it – what we do with his possessions, and that sort of thing. And then you got into the mess or you got into the car and went off to a favourite pub and had a good session. It was a way of, sort of, not dwelling on it. You could not afford to, I suppose, because otherwise you could have got like the guys that suffered from 'lack of moral fibre'. You just had to get on with it. It was happening all the time.

One of the awful things was when I was a flight commander, on more than one occasion I had to attend the funeral of one of the guys, you know the body was picked up out at sea or something like that. On at least one occasion I had to go and see the widow, who maybe had a small child, and

Philip and his MG sports car, which he bought for £10 in early 1942. PHILIP STEWART COLLECTION

break the news to them and return the possessions of the guy. That was tough, and that did affect your morale because you saw the effect on the next of kin. And that was the sort of thing it was better to keep away from, you needed to be harder than that, you needed to keep free of that sort of thing and just concentrate on the job that you were supposed to be doing. But the loss of close friends on the squadron hit. It almost affects one more now than it did then, when you think back on it.

The closest Philip came to losing his own life was late one afternoon in April 1942, when he was flying with 129 Squadron.

We were on a sortie over the French coast and we got involved in a battle. We were actually escorting some bombers, I think, and there was an attack. There was anti-aircraft fire coming up from the French coast, and whether I was hit by that or whether I was hit by an enemy aircraft I really don't know. The only thing was, we got completely broken up and I found myself entirely on my own and then realised that I had been hit. The engine was playing up so I made it back towards the English coast. I thought I was going to make it back to England and hopefully crash-land, but realised when I was – I don't know what, 12 or 14 miles out – there was no hope. The aircraft by then was well on fire, the engine was burning, there was smoke coming out in all directions. There were small flames and it was getting fairly hot too, so I thought I'd better get out. I left it a bit late, and by that time one of our pilots had caught up to me and he was screaming to me to get out. I got out and used my parachute, but it only just had time to open before I hit the sea. It broke my fall, which was lucky, but two moments later would have been too late.

The first thing you did was to get rid of the parachute, because that could drag you. Your dinghy was attached to you, it was clipped at the bottom of the parachute. But that came away very quickly and easily once the parachute was released, and the force of the tide or the current in the water pulled the parachute away. I inflated my dinghy and inflated my Mae West [life jacket] once I was in the water. It was pretty rough and it was early evening, April I think it was. But it was getting dark. I could see cliffs. You had a whistle on you and you blew that. I can't remember doing much else.

In spite of fading light, the crew of a patrolling air-sea rescue launch on its way back to shore saw the parachute coming down and turned back to look for it. Shocked

Airmen practise manoeuvring their life-saving dinghies on the placid waters of the Avon River near Ibsley, Hampshire, 1943. Such a dinghy helped save Philip Stewart's life when he was shot down in the English Channel. PHILIP STEWART COLLECTION

and freezing, Philip was picked up. He reckons he would not have survived the night because of the cold. Within 24 hours he was flying again. His ordeal won him places in the RAF's Caterpillar Club, whose members had parachuted to safety with the aid of silk, and the Goldfish Club for those 'escaping death by use of emergency dinghy'.

In April 1943 Philip joined 616 Squadron and was promoted to command a flight. From this time until just before D-Day, the main task of the squadrons was 'intruding' – going behind enemy lines to destroy strategic targets. This required fast, low-level flying to avoid enemy radar. Philip disliked low flying over the sea because planes sometimes crashed into the water. And once over land, and under cloud, low flying brought other challenges.

> Well it's not only trickier, it's also very difficult to find your targets travelling at the speed that the Spitfire flew at, looking for a specific railway line or something like that. If you are at a very low level, you are travelling so fast you could pass over the thing before you know whether you have reached it. So by the time you turn and come back the train you've seen

might have disappeared. So you have to fly at a reasonable height to spot your target. These could be various things such as transport on the roads, because it was always assumed that any lorries would have to be German because there was no petrol for civilians in France any more than there was in England. We similarly would attack trains if they appeared to be troop trains, which they virtually only were. We also tried to attack aerodromes and shoot up aircraft that were sitting on the ground, a surprise attack, which was the sort of thing they did in turn to us of course. You attacked them until they blew up. You would make absolutely certain that they weren't going to get mobile again.

We did a lot of gun practice. At times when we weren't busy on operations we used to go out to the shooting ranges on the coast. There were targets set up and we did a lot of gunnery practice, shooting at them with both cannon and machine gun. So it was a skill that you learnt from practice.

Did you have any sense of satisfaction when you got a hit?

Oh definitely, yes. Probably a few shouts of 'Whacko!' over the RT.

And when you were going in and were hitting a truck or a train – any thought of it having people inside?

No. You didn't worry about that. You couldn't. I saw guys falling out of a truck into ditches and so on when we'd started shooting, but we just carried on. I mean, your orders were to destroy the vehicle if possible, the same with the train, the locomotives, and in a way it was quite fun if you thought about the vehicle. I suppose one might possibly have thought, well I hope that they get out, but I don't think we did. I think by that stage, with the destruction we'd seen and the pilots we'd lost and all that had happened, there was an intense hate for the Germans, which I never lost. It had become personal. One's got to admit that, certainly. And of course it became much more so when one heard about the concentration camps. I've never been able to forgive the Germans.

As flying officers, Philip and his fellow pilots enjoyed living conditions that were in stark contrast to the grim reality of each day's work, and to the conditions experienced by servicemen in other forces. Many privately owned homes were requisitioned by the RAF.

Philip's fellow officers relax at a private home in Port Lympne, Kent. Like many it was requisitioned by the RAF during the Second World War for officers' accommodation.

PHILIP STEWART COLLECTION

We had really quite luxurious accommodation. One lovely one was one I was in when I was with 129. That was a very beautiful thatched-roof country house, beautiful garden. We were there in the spring and there were masses of azaleas and daffodils and bluebells and things, a lovely, lovely old house. Unfortunately it was a time when we were losing pilots hand over fist and it was a grim time, but it was a most beautiful place to go back to and relax in the time that you had off.

The most memorable one I suppose was later on when I was with No. 1 Squadron, it was called Port Lympne, it was built for Sir Phillip Sassoon, a banker. The house was huge, an extraordinary place and most elaborate inside. The dining room was panelled with lapis lazuli and it had rather rude friezes above the panelling. The main living room, a huge room, had a gold-leaf ceiling and there was an inner courtyard. Churchill used to stay there, and Lady Astor and people like that before the war. It had wonderful gardens, overlooking the sea on the coast. It was a most elaborate place.

It was not only living quarters that provided the young pilots with a break from their dangerous work. Philip describes the lifestyle he enjoyed on leave as 'unreal' in comparison with flying, and still reflects on the 'bizarre' contrast between this and the hours he spent fighting a war.

It was weird. It was very odd indeed. We were very busy indeed, and then maybe you got a 48-hour pass. What the majority of us used to do was head for London, because that's where the bright lights were and there was a bit of activity. So you'd go to London, and you'd book into a hotel and you'd lead a very good life indeed during that time. We had money. We were reasonably well paid. I for example booked into the Savoy, which was about the most expensive hotel in London, on one occasion. And you could eat out well.

The theatres were still operating, and there was quite a lot of bombing going on at that time, and if a raid started then somebody would come on stage and announce there was an air raid on, leave if you wish to, but the performance would carry on and the majority of the people stayed there. Sometimes you realised that something had landed fairly close, but I think the majority of the people just decided to stay put because otherwise by the time you made for an air-raid shelter it might be too late. It was better to sit there and hope.

The Windmill theatre, the famous Windmill girls where they posed absolutely motionless, naked from the waist up, they were popular and we used to trot along there.

I met up with people like Anna Neagle, who was a very well-known actress at that time, a film star, and her husband. Anna Neagle gave me a birthday party at a famous restaurant in Covent Garden. She was a charming person, very beautiful. It was incredible the sort of people one became involved with who you would have been very unlikely to have met had it not been for the war.

Did you find it hard going back after leave in London? Did you ever think, hell, I wish I didn't have to?

No, I didn't consciously. You just got used to it because you had an awful lot of those visits, an awful lot of times when you had those 48-hour passes and so on. It became automatic.

Back in the air, the long hours and dangerous work were beginning to take their toll.

I was desperately tired, I can remember that. I remember I'd sleep like mad but I would wake up tired. It was obvious, in the end, that I was reaching a stage where it was becoming a bit dangerous for me to be flying

Philip Stewart (foreground) and a fellow officer catch sleep where they can during a rest period at base. PHILIP STEWART COLLECTION

on active service. I had a fairly long stretch before I had a rest, and that was something they had to be very careful of because it could become dangerous. It wasn't the number of months but it was the number of actual sorties you'd done.

At what point would you have made the decision to talk to someone about it and say, 'Look, I don't think I should be doing this'?

I didn't. And I think sometimes some pilots should have done and didn't. You were, well you were diffident about it, thought you might lose face or something like that – I'm not going to admit that I'm not fit. But I was aware myself that I needed a break.

In mid-October 1943 Philip was sent on 'rest' to instruct pilots at a Spitfire Operational Training Unit (OTU). But a month later, while visiting his old squadron, he was injured when an American jeep he was travelling in crashed. He spent the next five months in hospital before he was able to return to instructing, time off that meant loss of rank.

Just four days before D-Day Philip was posted to command a flight on No. 1 Squadron. By then he was aware of an air of impatience, not only among his fellow servicemen but also in the civilian population. Everyone was waiting for the Allies to invade France and begin the last phase of the war. It soon became obvious to him that D-Day was close.

> It was partially because of the intense activity, particularly amongst the American forces, and the number of convoys there were on the roads. There was a big build-up going on. I think my first indication that it was very imminent was flying down from Red Hill to Predannack [RAF station] to join No. 1 Squadron, and flying over areas where every paddock was full of gliders. They had a special marking on them, black and white stripes, and they were obviously nose to tail ready just to be hauled off. Amazing quantities of them, and at the same time the roads were chock-a-block with convoys and so on.

Two nights before D-Day all the pilots on the squadron were alerted that the invasion was close.

> The following day the invasion fleet appeared and were patrolling up and down off the coast, and we could see them very, very clearly. Just hundreds and hundreds and hundreds of ships of all sizes and descriptions, from battleships down to quite small merchant vessels which were carrying troops as well. Just an incredible fleet. Because of weather conditions they were delayed for one day, and the whole of that day they were just cruising up and down the coast, and our officers' quarters were the hotel on the cliffs above and we had a very good view straight out to sea. We had an absolute grandstand view, incredible.

As with all briefings, the squadron was only told on the morning of D-Day itself what they would be doing. Flying towards France the planes passed over thousands of vessels in the Channel.

> I can remember looking down on the ships which were crossing. It took them a long time to get the whole lot over, and in a lot of them the troops were out on deck, or they were in landing craft which were completely open. I had a feeling of excitement, a realisation that at last something was happening and it was on a tremendous scale. I'm aware that one was part of something which involved many thousands of people and an enormous

amount of planning, and also that if it failed it would be a complete disaster, so it had to succeed. You were aware of that. Aware that any role you undertook was more important than ever before. If you were asked to do some particular job, well then you must endeavour your utmost to make sure that you succeeded.

The poor weather which had delayed D-Day had improved only a little on 6 June. Low cloud hampered the job that No. 1 Squadron set out to do, but it did not fully protect enemy transport targets.

We only had one sortie on D-Day, and that I think was due to weather conditions. We flew to the Vannes area in France. We destroyed one train on the way in which blew up, and another one on the way out, so we claimed two locomotives. We also attacked a staff car which was on the road. We destroyed it, and it was then that I was obviously shot at by soldiers, because when I came back I found a 303 bullet in the seat and another through the wing. I thought it extraordinary. Of course it wasn't hard enough for me to have felt anything, and it was my ground crew that discovered it after I landed. They came to me and said, 'You've got a couple of bullet holes.' It didn't affect the aircraft's flying ability. They were able to patch up the holes. Just thank goodness the seat is armour-plated.

After D-Day the job of No 1. Squadron was far from over. It continued to fly over enemy territory, destroying transport and other strategic targets. And there was a new threat for fighter pilots to conquer. They were intent on intercepting V1 flying bombs, or doodlebugs, aimed at London.

Flying bombs were easy to catch in a way in that our speed was far greater than theirs, but the fact that they were travelling comparatively slowly made it difficult to pull up to shoot at them. You'd come at them, and trying to attack these things which were moving along slower than you were in the air was not all that easy. Some guys, it was reported, even managed to put one of the wings of their Spitfire or whatever they were flying under the wing of the bomb and tip it over, and then that upset its gyrocompass and it would crash. But there was also a risk that it would explode, and one or two fighters were blown up like that.

There were an enormous number of them. We shot down a lot, in fact we shot down so many in the Detling area, which was just outside

An RAF Spitfire edges into position beside a V1 flying bomb to tip its wing and alter its course, August 1944. IMPERIAL WAR MUSEUM, CH 16280

Maidstone, that we had a deputation from the mayor and councillors asking us to kindly stop shooting them down over Maidstone because the population was becoming hysterical. But our orders were, at all costs don't let them get to London.

There were some extraordinary incidents. I remember very well being off duty. We were in the mess, we had beers in hand, and we heard V1s coming over. They made such a noise, their motor was very distinctive. There was also an air-raid warning given and we realised they were coming over the aerodrome, and we went out and there were Typhoons from another base chasing them, two Typhoon fighters. And they didn't succeed in shooting one down and they got near the balloon barrage, which we could see very clearly because we were right on the Thames Estuary and you could see the balloon barrage over London from where we were – and this thing hit the cable, spun round, and then it was coming back with these guys deciding to go back to base – they were flying along with this thing behind them, and we were shouting out, 'Look behind you! Look behind you!' And suddenly they spotted it and then they turned round and shot it down.

The civilians, I think, were becoming desperately tired. The V1s had had an enormous effect, and then there were the V2s, which were even more terrifying and which nothing could be done about, and that had a big effect on morale. So I don't think there was much elation, it was almost like holding your breath and thinking, Can this be it? Are we actually going to succeed now? The job was still going on, we were still losing pilots.

In Philip's final months of operational flying, No 1. Squadron was flying to Holland and Belgium and staying in quarters there. There was no let-up from their work. The longest leave Philip had had was one week. The squadron was flying more than it had since 1942.

Philip's final flight as a fighter pilot was on 26 April 1945. Having flown a total of 749 operational flying hours in Spitfires, he was disappointed that at the time he was unaware that this would be his last operational flight. On VE Day he was on leave in London.

I joined the vast crowds that thronged around where Churchill came out on the balcony, and then up to Buckingham Palace and saw the royal family come out and took part in the celebrations there. Tremendous feelings. Overwhelmed really . . . you were propelled around by the crowd, almost lifted off your feet, the crowds were so dense and they were moving. And the excitement and the general elation was tremendous.

After the war Philip Stewart came home and married Barbara Thomson, who had been a WAAF in New Zealand during the war. The couple lived for many years in Yorkshire, where their children were born and Philip worked in the wool trade and later in publishing and bookselling. The Stewarts retired to Christchurch in 1980.

Philip was mentioned in despatches for distinguished service during the war. He reflects on those years with mixed feelings.

I suppose one shouldn't say it, but one has some sense of pride that you took part and you did something that was worthwhile. Sadness that it was

Philip Stewart, 2004.
ALISON PARR

not the war to end all wars, that there is no such thing. In fact to my mind the world is in a far worse state than it was then. There was never a truer word than when, after September 11, somebody said the world will never be the same again. So a sense of disappointment that we went through that, loads of people went through that, loads of lives were lost and yet no way was it a war to end all wars.

Terry Scott, 1943. TERRY SCOTT COLLECTION

Terry Scott

LEADING SEAMAN, HMS *LAWFORD*, RN

Having Sid to look after did make a difference. I couldn't worry about myself and not Sid. I had to think of us both.

Terry Scott was born in Cromwell in Central Otago in 1921. His father worked as a blacksmith and gold miner, and Terry walked four miles each day to primary school in Bannockburn. In this landlocked area, he and his friends spent hot summer days swimming in a cattle watering hole. Just after D-Day, this childhood fun would help to save his life.

> At Bannockburn there was a farmer who had cows, and he had a dam that he'd built for irrigation purposes, just made with soil. If there was water in it we were allowed to go down and swim. And that's where I learnt to swim. All I could do was dog-paddle, and then I learned to breaststroke. My grandmother lived down on the Kawarau River. We'd go down to my grandmother's for Sunday dinner and then Dad would take us down to the river to have a swim. There was a pond there and Mum was scared of it – you could see her sitting on a stone on the side, praying that we wouldn't get drowned. I'd see her cross herself and I think she had her rosary beads. She was scared of the water. I wasn't – I could dog-paddle across those ponds just as quick as any of the others.

After three years at Cromwell District High School, Terry became a cadet with New Zealand Railways, working on local stations. He was living in Middlemarch when he joined up with the navy. The close-knit rural communities of Central Otago gave gifts to their departing sons – Terry received two engraved gold watches, one each from the people of Middlemarch and Bannockburn.

Terry Scott with his fiancée, Evelyn Howell, against the dry hills of Central Otago, 1943.
TERRY SCOTT COLLECTION

All the country places, they always gave them a dance and a send-off. It was good but the parents were always weeping. Like at Bannockburn, I'd see Mum weeping and there'd be somebody else having a weep and it made it sad. But at the same time we were pleased we were on final leave. I got a send-off at both Middlemarch and Bannockburn. At Middlemarch there was a piano, a violin and an accordion, and they were great for dancing to. All the songs of that day. I loved dancing. You never went to a dance without a supper either at Bannockburn or at Middlemarch – always sandwiches and cakes.

It was very hard to see the mothers weeping. I'd go to somebody else's send-off and see a mother weeping, and even Dad shed a few tears when I left. I can always remember, when I left I had to go to Dunedin by train

Young recruits learn to scrub the decks on HMS *Philomel*, 1940. At the beginning of his service Terry Scott spent a short time here before being sent to a coastal watch station in Northland. ROYAL NEW ZEALAND NAVY MUSEUM, AAC0028

from Cromwell, my parents came and I can always remember Dad took it very hard. I can still see him walking up the platform at the Cromwell railway station, and I'm sure he was having a weep. It was hard saying goodbye to anybody, because in country areas they'd give you a kiss for any good reason and I found it very hard.

Terry spent three months on a coastal watch station in Northland, then some time on HMS *Leander* before sailing for the United Kingdom in November 1943. He was posted as an ordinary seaman to HMS *Lawford*, one of hundreds of frigates built that year in the United States and loaned to the Royal Navy. When his friend Eric Leith joined the *Lawford* with him they became the only two New Zealanders on board.

It was a very fragile ship. In fact a boat came alongside one day and bumped it, and it put a dent in the hull. It was just built for the invasion. Eric said,

'Scottie, I don't think this one would take much to put her down', and I said, 'Well, we've just got to put up with it.' His brother George was over in England, and he came and saw us one day, and after he'd gone Eric said to me, 'George is not very happy with us being on this ship. He said it wouldn't take much to break it up.' Then one day he came out and said, 'I've been speaking to the writer' – that's the staff clerk – 'and he said you and I are on draft', I think it was back to New Zealand. And I said, 'Oh hell no, Eric, we're on here now, I'd like to see it through.'

Terry made friends with a seaman in the RDF (radar) office and spent most of his time there. He got used to the comparative formality of the British navy and took to life at sea. At one stage a petty officer talked him into growing a beard.

I think he had a nice little beard himself. And of course when you grow a beard in the navy you have to go before the captain, so he said, 'Come on Scottie, what about it?' And I said, 'Oh alright, if you think so.' And he

HMS *Lawford*, Terry Scott's ship. IMPERIAL WAR MUSEUM, A 21817

rounded up about six or seven of us. We're all waiting outside the captain's office in a small room. Then you're taken in to face the captain. I think the petty officer was the one who read out the request, 'Ordinary Seaman Scott requests permission to discontinue shaving, sir.' The captain said to me, 'Do you think you can grow a beard, Scott?' And I said, 'Yes, sir.' Request granted. They don't turn you down.

Terry was never in a hurry when the daily tot of navy rum was served to the men.

> They piped for rum bosuns, and then, 'All hands to the rum bosun.' I never took rum when I was on board. Probably the fact that I wanted the money, because if you didn't take rum you got 3d a day extra. The only time I took rum was when we knew we were going to D-Day – going to war – I think perhaps to steady my nerves, but I still never drank much of it.
>
> I don't know what I'd be like if I had to pick up a rifle and shoot a person. I found it much easier being in the navy; we weren't fighting men, we were fighting ships and that was our main target. If we saw a German walking along we wouldn't grab a gun and shoot him, but if there was a German ship about we do our damnedest to sink it.

In the cramped conditions below deck on the *Lawford*, the men slept closely together. They seldom used their hammocks but instead threw mattresses on the floor. Terry had one friend in particular who slept beside him.

> My head was at his feet – Sid Copeland, an Englishman. I liked him very much. He was a good guy to get on with when we were off duty, if we were sitting in the mess deck. I found him a very good chap. We talked mainly about New Zealand, about back home. I was never a good one at making conversation, but he was excellent. I could sit and talk to him. He became quite a close friend. I got on with him very well.

As D-Day approached the tension mounted on the *Lawford*.

> I think there was a general restlessness, because we didn't know what was happening and there were rumours that we'd be sailing tonight, and then we'd perhaps wake up and the ship was still there. You know, probably a case of a bit more bitching at each other, if you don't mind me using that word, and we wanted action. We knew when action was going to come.

We knew things were getting near then. Then one day we looked up and here were these massive big blocks of concrete being towed towards the Channel, and nobody knew what they were. There was all sorts of guessing. But that was a Mulberry Harbour.

I think there was quite a feeling, what's going to happen to us? What have we got in the future? We'd seen the huge harbour concrete blocks and we thought things must be coming right. Eric Leith turned to me and he said, 'Well you've had your way, Scottie' – that was the night before we sailed. The weather was not very good, the forecast was bad but they said they couldn't delay it any longer, we had to go. We weren't told anything. I think it was after we sailed that the captain called, 'Attention!', he was going to address us. And over the loudspeaker he said we're heading for the French coast. I suppose I felt a bit emotional. I wonder if I'll ever see home again. And I probably shed a few tears on our way across.

I think there was sort of a general feeling, this is it. That seemed to be going through the whole ship's company, and we knew something was going to happen. I think underneath we were probably all a bit scared. You didn't know what was going to happen to you.

We weren't very far from the coast. We could see all these other ships coming across, landing craft, and they were just like big black blobs of paper, here, there and everywhere.

On D-Day the *Lawford* was stationed off Juno Beach. Two days after taking position, the ship received what was to be its final order.

That night we got a call to go and frighten some E-boats off – we weren't concerned about sinking them because they were so fast they'd get away from us anyhow, but it was to keep them away from the area where things were happening. Once the E-boats saw us, they just took off and that was all we were concerned with, to get them out of the way. We were coming back, we were almost back to our station I would think, so we were not far from where we were going to drop anchor, and Eric Leith and I were in a little radar cabin. And I was just starting to doze and Eric was on watch and there was a bump . . . a thud, and I jumped and Eric said, 'We've been hit, Scottie.' I said, 'What?' He said, 'We've been hit. Don't panic, Scottie', and I said, 'I'm OK.'

And of course in the navy you don't ever take anything on yourself, you report a thing and then wait for instructions. So he called up to the bridge – 'Radar to bridge, radar to bridge' – and they acknowledged it and said,

'Just hold your stations and wait for further orders'. There were quite a few minutes, and a minute seemed like an hour, and yet I wasn't frightened. I don't know why, because I'm not brave. We just sat there dumb for a few minutes, and then we got, 'Prepare to abandon ship' – and that was when it really hit us. It was almost just breaking daylight. It was still dark, but you could see just so far ahead of you.

Were there any lights going on the ship at all?

No, not that I was aware of.

So the ship itself was in darkness?

Yes. We got, 'Proceed to abandon ship stations', so we walked out – there was no sense in trying to rush it. We went down the ladder and along to the stern, that was our abandon ship station. Every sailor has an area which he proceeds to if you're going to lose your ship.

This engineer officer said, 'How are you, Scottie?' And I said, 'I'm OK, sir.' He said, 'Look, I've got one here pretty badly hit, could you help him off?' I said, 'I'll look after him, sir.' And it was Sid Copeland, the chap that I was sleeping beside. He'd got his legs smacked. I got quite a shock – the fact that we'd slept so closely together and that we'd got to know each other well. I said, 'Come with me, Sid, and I'll look after you.'

Having Sid to look after did make a difference. I couldn't worry about myself and not Sid. I had to think of us both. He said, 'Look, Scottie, you just push me over the side and you save yourself.' I said, 'You'll come over with me', and I think I put my arm round him, and when I felt it was time to get off the ship I said, 'Come on, Sid.' I said, 'We'll jump.' Once we hit the water I couldn't hold onto him and he got washed round the stern of the ship and I didn't. I was quite a bit behind him, but I could sense there were some others round the stern of the ship that would probably catch him – I could pick out they were sailors.

I thought, well, every man for himself. I looked over and I could see a ship. I thought it was a minesweeper and it was some distance away, and I thought, well, I've got my life jacket – I knew I had my heavy boots on, but I thought, as long as I can stay afloat, I'll get there. So I started off swimming. I don't know if I ever looked back at the ship. I don't think I did. I didn't feel cold, and of course I had my big mechanics' overalls on – we always had those on when we were on watch, to keep us warm and in case

Terry Scott was not the only lucky sailor during Operation Neptune. Survivors from a torpedoed landing craft are helped on board a rescuing ship, June 1944. IMPERIAL WAR MUSEUM, A 23971

of emergency. That probably hindered me a bit, but once I left the *Lawford* I knew it would be quite a long swim. I think it was probably about three-quarters of an hour. For some reason I wasn't frightened. I think you don't get so scared when you know there's everybody for themselves. I had my life jacket on. I might have been a bit scared occasionally, but I was too intent on swimming to that one ship.

And when I got reasonably close I could see some of them had got on the ship, and when I got there they lowered a rope to me and I got about halfway up and I slipped and went down. I had to climb up again. I climbed up and the chap at the top, he had a jar of rum – he said, 'Come on Scottie, get this down you.' And he handed me a glass with quite a bit of rum in it and I swallowed it down.

When they got me on board my first words were, 'Do you know if Copeland's been saved.' And somebody said, 'I think he might be down in sick bay', and so they told me where to go. I went down there and Sid was there – every time I think of it I go into tears – there wasn't a word spoken and he put his arms out. Sid and I both had a bit of a cry. He put his arms round me and we squeezed and then we came to.

Thirty-seven men from the *Lawford* died that night. The official explanation for the ship's sinking was that it was hit by a German aircraft. Divers have subsequently suggested the ship was hit underwater, from beneath.

The ship that picked up Terry and some other *Lawford* survivors was the HMS *Scylla*, a cruiser. Terry still had his boots on when he reached the ship, but was soon parted from them.

A page from Terry Scott's scrapbook, containing a letter from Sid Copeland to his mate 'Scottie', written from hospital in July 1944. Included are the words: 'We all had a severe shaking pal, and as you no doubt know I thought my time had come. A man can't, and just doesn't, say "thank you", he hopes to live on and await the day when he can do a similar thing for his comrade. I guess you know what I mean.' TERRY SCOTT COLLECTION

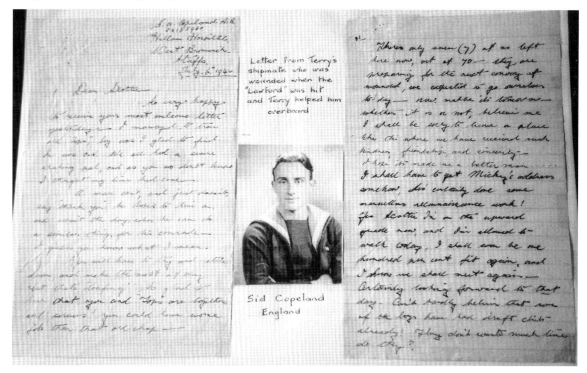

On the *Scylla* a sailor said to me, 'When we get back to England you'll get a complete outfit of clothing. If you give me your boots and I give you my old ones, you'll get all new clothes when you get back on to English soil. I'll be able to put these in and get a new pair.' War wasn't worrying him, you see.

Did you have the same size feet?

No, mine were too big for him, I think. I wasn't suffering any, because they were wet boots anyhow.

Back in the United Kingdom, Terry had some leave and visited friends of his family in Scotland.

I think it helped me settle down. The daughter's boyfriend, he was there. He was in the air force and he had had to crash-land just a few hundred

Terry Scott, 2004. ALISON PARR

yards from his airbase, and I think he was pretty lucky to get out of it. We didn't talk much about that, in fact we didn't talk much about the ship either, but he said, 'Come on, I'll take you into some friends in the village.' Of course we had to have a whisky with them. They would have fed me with whisky all day if I'd wanted it. But I had a drink with them. It was funny, I sort of felt lost, very much so.

Terry spent another year in the Royal Navy, including some time at a base in Ceylon, now Sri Lanka. After the war he worked as a clerk for New Zealand Railways in Middlemarch, and later as an insurance salesman in Cromwell. In 1946 he married Evelyn Howell, who had served in the land army in New Zealand during the war. The couple remained in Cromwell and had four children. Terry still remembers his 1945 homecoming.

They gave me a bit of a welcome in the supper room of the hall at Middlemarch and the next day I caught the train to Cromwell. I can still see my mother running along under the veranda on the platform and putting her arms round me, and Dad was elated. And then Dad said, 'I'll take you in to the middle pub and give you a drink' – there were three pubs in Cromwell at that time, top, middle and bottom – and so we had one drink. There was a welcome-home dance for us at Bannockburn. Everybody was happy, everyone was smiling.

Don Sisley, 1940. DON SISLEY COLLECTION

Don Sisley

FLIGHT LIEUTENANT, 22 SQUADRON AND 233 SQUADRON, RAF

Chaos. The beach was littered with sunken ships and beach
obstacles. After the initial assault it was a mess.

DON SISLEY WAS BORN IN INGLEWOOD IN 1921. HIS FATHER HAD BEEN BADLY wounded at Gallipoli, but in spite of this began breaking in a farm in Taranaki, part of a rehabilitation scheme for First World War veterans. The Depression forced the family off the land and tough times followed. Don wanted to go to university but that was out of the question financially. When the Second World War broke out he was working as a clerical cadet in the State Advances Corporation. He had no doubts about which service he wanted to join.

> I wanted to be in the air force. I've always been interested in flying. I was at New Plymouth airport the day Kingsford Smith landed in 1928. I was seven. It was a great day. The Southern Cross, it was a wonderful old machine, and when he arrived and circled round the grass field there was a huge crowd waiting to greet him, and it was just fantastic when this great big three-motored monster touched down. Yeah, I'll never forget that day. There was cheering, clapping, shouting – it was amazing.

After some training in New Zealand, Don left in 1940 for Canada and the Empire Air Training Scheme. Operational training followed in England, and from there a posting as a navigator to 22 Squadron, a torpedo bomber unit. With this squadron he served in England, the Middle East, Malta and Ceylon (Sri Lanka), where he was based for sixteen months. He remembers that a wing commander had borrowed a pet lion cub from Colombo zoo. The animal slept with him and accompanied him on trips to the beach.

New Zealand airmen take a break from their journey across Canada, on their way to take part in the Empire Air Training Scheme, 1941. LES MUNRO COLLECTION

Alongside the quirks of foreign service, the grim reality of combat flying was part of daily life. Like most airmen of the time, Don had his first experience of loss while he was still training. In one case, an entire crew was killed in a crash. But even at that stage, the survivors were learning not to dwell on tragedy.

Well, you couldn't let it affect you too much. We would sort of half joke about it. Talk about them going for a burton and this kind of thing – if you started to worry about the losses you wouldn't get anywhere. It was the same all the way through. We all knew every time we flew there was danger involved. But you can't let that sort of thing stop you. You had to be fatalistic. We were a lot better off than the poor sods in Bomber Command, for instance. They had horrendous losses during the war.

All operations were exciting. Every time you went on an operational flight there was something, there was some weird sort of attraction about

Dakotas like this one were used extensively by the RAF to transport troops and supplies during Operation Overlord. AIR FORCE MUSEUM, CHRISTCHURCH

it. You know you're sticking your neck out and yet you still do it. I suppose it's like people go bungy jumping, which I wouldn't, but the people that do must get a kick out of it. They wouldn't do it otherwise, would they? Danger is part of the attraction.

In March 1944 Don was moved to 233 Squadron, part of the Second Tactical Air Force set up to prepare for the invasion of France. The squadron flew Dakotas, and their role in Operation Overlord would be to tow gliders and carry and drop paratroops into France.

Each plane had a crew of four – pilot, navigator, wireless operator and, Don's new role, map reader. His task was to ensure they flew the correct track over enemy territory by feeding the navigator information about key places, such as turning points. For nearly three months leading up to D-Day, the squadron trained intensively at their base at Blakehill Farm, Wiltshire.

We were quite excited about it. At last we felt we were going to do something worthwhile. The training consisted of circuits and landings, formation flying, navigation exercises and glider towing, and day and night paratroop dropping. When we were glider-towing we had to see that the glider was taken to the landing zone and then the pilots would just do a circuit round and the glider pilot would release when he wanted to.

We'd been doing circuits and bumps, and I thought I'd try it from the glider end. The pilot was a flight sergeant: I just asked him, I said, 'Would you mind if I came for a trip in the glider.' He said, 'No, you're welcome.' Although they're called gliders, that's a misnomer really – they don't glide, they drop like a stone, and the pilot has to be very skilled at picking the right moment to release the glider from the towing aircraft and, allowing for wind direction and so forth, to get down on to the desired spot on the ground. So it's not easy. There's no noise. You're sitting up above the towing aircraft to keep out of the slipstream. There's just the sound of the air passing. It's harder for the glider pilot than the towing pilot. But the Dakotas coped quite well with towing the gliders.

What was the release like?

The pilot just selected the correct moment to release and the tow rope just went away, and the nose of the glider went down at a very steep angle, 'cos they're quite heavy aircraft. Then once we got near the ground – the gliders have got control surfaces the same as an aeroplane, a rudder and so forth, so he's got control – and he just levelled off and landed on the runway. The landing zones for the gliders in Normandy were pretty rough. And the Germans had put up great things like telegraph poles on some of the fields that had been selected, so changes had to be made. Some of the gliders crashed on landing. It was a bit chaotic really.

Don's main responsibility as map reader was to see that paratroops were dropped on the right spot, the drop zone. The intensive training in the lead-up to D-Day was not only for the Dakota crews – it was also for the paratroops themselves.

A lot of them hadn't done much actual dropping before they came to live at Blakehill Farm, and it was pretty concentrated. We did day drops, night drops, in various parts of southern England. I've never used a parachute, so I can't imagine what it was like, but it's not the sort of job that appealed to me greatly. I wouldn't have wanted to be a paratrooper. Targets. They were human targets for the Germans on the ground, weren't they? Not very nice. I felt sorry for them, really. I admired them but I thought, what the hell inspires them to do this? 'Cos they were all volunteers in the paras. They got more pay, I think that was the inducement.

Did you ever talk with any of them about why they did it?

With a few of them, yeah. They were drawn from all parts of the British Army into the para brigades, and their motives all differed I suppose. Some of them were sick of doing nothing and wanted some more excitement, more pay, glamour. There's a certain amount of glamour attached to wearing the para wings. They were all young blokes – late teens and early twenties. Adventurous types.

What sense of responsibility did you all have?

Oh, tremendous, tremendous. As D-Day approached we were briefed on the 3rd of June by a very high-powered briefing team – General Browning, who was head of the British Airborne Forces at the time, and Air Chief Marshal Tedder, Eisenhower's deputy. They came to Blakehill Farm. They explained in some detail the overall plan for the invasion. They showed us film of the run in from the coast to our drop zones – film which had been taken by photographic reconnaissance Spitfires, I think. They showed that at various speeds, and over and over again we were shown that film. I had a look at it again several times, because there were two full days from the briefing until the operation. You had to have it firmly fixed in your mind what you were going to be looking at. It didn't prove to be much use in the event because of the weather on the night.

After a day's postponement because of weather, conditions were still not ideal when the squadron finally took off for France with nearly 600 soldiers of the Fifth Parachute Regiment from the Sixth Airborne Division. More than 100 of them were carried in gliders, the rest in Dakotas.

In Don's plane were nineteen paratroops. Their drop zone was close to the city of Caen – their initial task, to blow up a bridge across the River Orne to prevent German armour getting to the beachhead. Don remembers how he felt when the time came for the beginning of their part in the long-awaited invasion.

It was exciting. The adrenalin was pumping because we knew that something pretty important was happening. We took off at 23.15 on the fifth of June and were airborne for three hours. We'd be chatting and

Paratroops and crew waiting to board their plane for France on the eve of D-Day. IMPERIAL WAR MUSEUM, H 39071

talking to the troops at the back on the way over. We wished them good luck and good drop. I shook hands with Major Wilson – he was their leader. He was a great bloke.

What were your thoughts about the weather conditions?

We knew it was going to be difficult to find the drop zone. But all you can do is hope for the best. And the paratroops knew that too. We explained to them that we'll try and get you as close as possible, but there are no guarantees. They were quite happy about that. It was pretty tense. They were looking forward to something not exactly pleasant. They were amazingly cheerful, but you could feel the pressure – that they were feeling under pressure, and who could blame them?

233 Squadron was flying in the dark and each pilot could see only the blue forma-tion-keeping lights on the aircraft in front of them. Before heading for the French coast, they had to join the rest of the airborne forces.

We didn't take off directly for the south coast. We had to fly north-west, if I remember rightly, for about half an hour, and join the stream of aircraft that was coming down towards the coast from other bases. There were thousands of planes whose movements had to be controlled and we had to be very precise about where we positioned ourselves, so this is where the flying skills and the navigation skills came in. But once we joined up with the main stream, we then turned south and crossed the coast at a place called Littlehampton and headed across to France from there.

On our way across the Channel, away to the south of us, we could see the American airborne force – they were lit up like a Christmas tree and we were all in darkness, but it didn't seem to worry them. I thought, they may be doing well at the moment, but wait for half an hour when they get near the coast and see what happens. And that is what happened. The German defences around Cherbourg took a heavy toll of them. The Americans asked for it, they were prime targets. They were scattered over a huge area of Brittany and Normandy, and there were far more Germans on the ground in that part of France than there were around Caen. I think the Germans around Caen were caught by surprise. They didn't think anyone would be stupid enough to try landing troops on a night like that. There was nothing like that affecting us where we were in Normandy. We were much further north. We knew we were part of a big stream and we were all familiar with the big bomber streams that used to go over regularly, and from the ground they sounded like an express train roaring away. It was an amazing sight to see Bomber Command taking off with a thousand bombers going to Cologne or somewhere.

We were all wearing flak suits and steel helmets. So they did give us that extra protection. It was just like a jerkin with no sleeves, and you pop it over your head and it was steel reinforcing – they were quite heavy to wear. In fact I didn't wear mine. I sat on mine. I thought it would be better protection. I thought any fire coming up from the ground was not going to hit my body or my head but other parts! I didn't fancy the flak suits greatly. I didn't think they were really necessary. I think the pilot was sitting on his too. We'd agreed we'd sit on ours and not wear them. And I had my flying helmet on as well as my steel helmet. We had Mae Wests [life jackets] on, too. Another thing with this type of work, the crew don't carry parachutes when you're doing paratrooping work, because you can't have a situation where the crew leave the aircraft and leave the paratroops to their own devices.

But you could have been hit flying back after the drop.

Mmm . . . we always looked on the bright side.

What do you remember of the rest of the flight to the drop zone that night?

We crossed the coast pretty well on track. I knew we were over the surf.
One of the things I had to do was drop a load of small bombs on the beach
as we went over to try and remove some of the beach obstacles, because
where we were crossing the coast was one of the beaches the troops were
going to land on. It must have been Sword Beach. So I did that just by
guess and by God. There was no proper bomb-aiming or anything like
that. We were down to about 500 feet all the way and we felt the explosion
when they went off. Whether they did any good or not, I don't know.
There was a fitful moon. But mainly the sky was cloudy, low cloud. Every
now and again you'd see a bit of moon, but there was not enough to see
by. It was so dark that we couldn't identify rivers and streams and buildings
and so forth on the ground. We were more or less blinded. We were doing
things without being able to see properly what we were doing.

So how on earth could you find where you were supposed to be going?

Well, we knew the flying time from where we crossed the coast to the
drop zone. And one of the features there was a peculiarly shaped wood
just close to the drop zone. So we just had to do it by dead reckoning. I
spotted this wood just to our port side, where it should have been, and I
gave the pilot the nod to put the green light on, and out they went. We
dropped the panniers at the same time. The other two aircraft behind
us did the same thing, and presumably the ones behind them. We were
quite happy. We'd done our best for them. There was no ground fire that
I could see.

That drop was just before 1 a.m., nearly two hours after take-off. Fifty years later,
Don spoke with a paratrooper who had been transported by 233 Squadron. He told
Don that after the drop the troops were distributed over a fair area.
     Immediately after the drop, there was no quick retreat from enemy territory for
the Dakota. Don and the crew had to continue further into France. Their troops
were the first to be dropped, so they had to keep going until the others completed
their missions, then sweep round and head back to England, crossing the coast near

Dunkirk. They got back to Blakehill Farm about 2.45 a.m. after flying for three and a half hours. After a short sleep, they were briefed for their next operation, named Rob Roy. Their task this time was to supply the troops with ammunition, blankets, food and medical supplies, all carried in panniers. For this operation, more than twenty aircraft from 233 Squadron were despatched.

> We identified the proper drop zone. There was a bit of action on the ground, but nothing very significant. There was small-arms fire coming up at us. It was obvious there was something going on on the ground. The weather was a bit better that night. You could see the ground and see the rivers. We were able to properly identify the drop zone.

However, the paratrooper who told Don about the successful drop on D-Day also reported that the Rob Roy operation did not go well – the Germans probably picked up most of the supplies dropped that night. And it was not only the drop itself that ended badly. As they passed over the Channel while returning to base, 40 Dakotas were shot at by Allied vessels. Eight from 233 Squadron were among those that went down.

> When we got back, we knew that some of the aircraft hadn't made it home from what was being said at the debriefing and so on, but we weren't given any details. We knew that there'd been trouble. We were told that some of the aircraft didn't make it. The thing was that the Allied ships knew we were going to be flying over them low, they knew what time we were going to be flying over them, and the trigger-happy gunners on the ships still opened up.

> *And these are unarmed planes?*

> Yeah. And a silhouette of a Dakota is unlike any German bomber. They must have known that there couldn't have been that many German bombers in a formation coming to assault them anyway. I can understand it in a way – they're very nervous, these ships' gunners. We used to call them trigger-happy. We've also been fired upon by anti-aircraft units in England, coming back at night.

> *So when the Dakotas were shot down, what was the reaction of the squadron?*

> Well, pretty uptight about it. It's just the fortunes of war.

In the weeks after D-Day, 233 Squadron continued to fly into France, transporting men and ammunition and bringing back the wounded. They were using temporary landing fields that often had little on the ground to identify them. Careful map reading meant scanning for roads, rivers, railways, towns, woods – any identifying feature. Don recalls crossing the Normandy coast on one of his first flights to France after D-Day.

> It was chaos. The beach was littered with sunken ships and beach obstacles. After the initial assault it was a mess. The troops had moved inland by then. There was unloading going on on the beaches. There was lots of activity on the beach, vehicles moving and people moving. There were a lot of people there in that small area.

Loading casualties onto an RAF Dakota in France for evacuation back to Britain, July 1944.
IMPERIAL WAR MUSEUM, B 6839

Were there a lot of ships, sunken ships or bits of ships that you could see?

Yeah, a helluva lot – landing craft mainly. Tank landing craft and infantry landing craft. They were just lying in the sand.

These ships had been sunk and then left high and dry when the tide went out. Just over two hours after landing in France, the squadron headed back to base. The Dakota they flew that day had been fitted up to carry stretchers, and it brought back wounded men from forward dressing stations.

We took off back to Blakehill with seventeen battle casualties on board. I think they were all British. We weren't very far from the battle front there, and we just hung around that aircraft until the ambulance rolled up with these people and they were onloaded. There were a few walking wounded. Most were stretcher cases though. We accepted it as part of what we were supposed to be doing. They weren't very talkative. I think they were just very relieved to be on their way back to England. Some of them had only been wounded a matter of a couple of hours before, so it was a pretty good service. On landing they were all very happy to be back in England. They were all smiles. All of them were heavily bandaged.

What was the airstrip like?

There were metal plates laid on the ground. Very temporary. You could hear the battle going on not too far away. Gunfire, bombs, big booms. Quite a lot of noise.

A few days later, on Don's 23rd birthday, the crew were off to another temporary landing strip in France, at Sainte Croix.

Our load was ten 500lb bombs, presumably for the Typhoons, the fighter bombers. That was only a fortnight after D-Day. The next trip was the 29th, we went to Bayeux with freight and we picked up nineteen wounded. We took a WAAF medical orderly with us, an English WAAF. She talked to them – actually they were allowed to smoke in the cabin, which is unusual, and she used to dish out cigarettes to them if they wanted them, and talk to them. Generally raise their morale. They were usually pretty girls – they seemed to be to me.

On one occasion we were on the ground for quite a while and this medical orderly and I decided to go for a stroll around the battlefield.

Don Sisley back home in New Zealand with his parents, Gordon and Ellen, in 1944. DON SISLEY COLLECTION

And we were mooching around. There were signs up, 'Achtung, Minen' [Attention, mines], and at one stage we came to a wheat field or barley field where there'd obviously been a battle. And all of a sudden there was a helluva stench, and we both sort of looked at each other and went a few paces further on and came across about three dead Germans, lying, rotting, decomposing in the field. They hadn't been picked up. So we skedaddled out of there pretty quick. It was obvious that a real battle had taken place – there were broken-down vehicles and burnt-out vehicles and so forth. So that did me for marching around the Normandy beachhead. She seemed a bit upset about it . . . a lot of the German troops in France were only kids.

Don returned to New Zealand in 1944 and worked in various management positions. He also served in the Territorial Army in the artillery for eleven years, achieving the rank of major. He has married three times and has three children.

Of the 30 young men with whom Don trained in Canada and then travelled to England, twelve were killed in service. On reflection, he considers his involvement in D-Day to have been among his best experiences.

Don Sisley, 2004.
ALISON PARR

I think that was the most satisfying, the most worthwhile. The best contribution that I made, I think, to the war effort. It was a big moment in the war. It was something that the world was waiting for and it was quite a buzz, really, at the time.

I don't take part in dawn services any more. I'm not a great one for parading around with my campaign medals. I spend Anzac Day thinking about my father's service and thinking about the guys who I went away from New Zealand with in the air force, and didn't come back.

George Wirepa, 1943. GEORGE WIREPA COLLECTION

George Wirepa

FLYING OFFICER, 514 SQUADRON, BOMBER COMMAND, RAF

But oh, it was a cruel war.

GEORGE WIREPA (NGATI MANIAPOTO) WAS BORN IN TE KUITI IN 1921. HIS father Thomas had served in the Pioneer Maori Battalion in Gallipoli and France in the First World War, in which he was one of five brothers to take part. He was wounded in both legs, and George remembers him wearing a brace.

George grew up on family land in the Waikato and went to secondary school at St Stephen's in Auckland. He was working as a railway porter in Auckland when he enlisted with the RNZAF. To prepare for training, he spent his evenings at night classes in maths at Auckland Grammar School. In November 1942 he left New Zealand for six months training as an air bomber in Canada. On arrival in England in July 1943 he expected to be posted to the New Zealand bomber squadron, No. 75. Instead he was sent to 514 Squadron because, he was told, they were short of bomb aimers. To do this job, George had to lie in the nose of a Lancaster, below the cockpit.

> I was lying on perspex. I went down a couple of steps and then I laid down there. I never used to go into my position until we took off because if the plane crashed on take-off, being in the nose you are gone, your chances of survival are nil. From there you could see everything, I used to see everything that was going on, you could see all the blinkin' flak coming up. On a daylight raid I used to map-read and call up the navigator and tell him we're flying over so and so. But at night-time, well if it was a full moon you could see the ground and the shape of the things, you get a fair idea where you are.

Flying Officer George Wirepa, right, with fellow New Zealand airmen in former world heavyweight boxing champion Jack Dempsey's restaurant, New York, 1943. They are on the way to England after training in Canada. GEORGE WIREPA COLLECTION

Bomb aimers also used astro-navigation, taking a fix on various stars, and later in the war had the aid of radar.

> Things became more sophisticated. They had what they called Pathfinders. They were the top crews of the Bomber Command. They used to mark the target, they used to drop green flares down, if those green flares were on target they used to drop red flares on top of it, and our job was to bomb those red flares. That's how it became in the latter part of the war. They were really on the ball. I didn't have to look for the target, just bomb those red flares. I released the bombs. When we got to the target area I instructed the pilot, 'Bomb doors open', and I switched on, 'All bombs alive', and then was giving instructions, 'Left, Left steady, Right steady', until we get over the target – press the tit and away she goes! If we were doing a daylight raid we could see the bombs going right down to the ground and exploding. But oh, it was a cruel war.

At the time George joined Bomber Command, the crews of 514 Squadron were among those making intensive raids on occupied and enemy territory, including

The round perspex window at the lower front of this Lancaster bomber is where bomb aimers such as George Wirepa lay to direct the aiming of bombs during raids. Ground crew are cleaning the plane between operations. IMPERIAL WAR MUSEUM, TR 188

many German cities. George would know where he was headed each night from the kind and quantity of bombs being loaded onto the planes.

> I used to go and see what the armourers used to do, what type of bombs they loaded on. Soon as I saw the containers – they hold four-pound sticks of incendiary bombs – as soon as I saw those going on, I knew it was over Germany. Then you see the 8000-pound bomb going on and all the incendiary bombs, I knew it was over Germany. It's going to be a hot flight tonight, I'd have thought to myself, because they used to give us a hot reception. You knew when you went to Germany there was plenty of ack-ack.
>
> It never used to worry me. You had to go there and you just hoped you'd get back. Of course, we never flew direct to the target, that's the trouble. Berlin might be about ten hours altogether, but if we flew direct we could have gone there, say, in six hours. But we would try and fool the Germans where we were going to bomb, otherwise we'd have all these mobile ack-ack waiting to greet us. 88-millimetre – they used to fire quite a shell, and they were semi-automatic. You'd see a flash, a reddish explosion and a big black puff of smoke hanging in the air. With searchlights waving around,

Bomber crews on a dispersal truck on their way to their aircraft before an operation. IMPERIAL WAR MUSEUM, D 4751

you'd see all these black puffs. But you don't worry about the black puffs – you know there's a spent shell. It's the ones you don't see that you worry about.

You'd see nothing but explosions all around you, and the searchlights. And as soon as we dropped our bombs we'd get the hell out of it. If the searchlights lock on you, if one locks onto you the whole lot lock on. You feel naked. You feel that the searchlight is going right through you and then you can see all the flak coming up at you. Well the idea then is to get out of the area as fast as you can. I can see some poor devil – he's got the searchlights locked onto him, got all the ack-ack concentrated on him, with the plane copping all the flak. I didn't have any feeling about those planes – you were just concerned about yourself, whether you're going to get through and get back. It's survival, yeah.

Being in the nose of the plane like that you must have felt incredibly vulnerable.

Well, the whole crew was vulnerable.

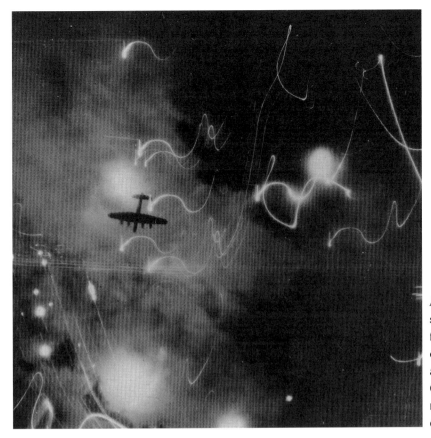

A Lancaster bomber
silhouetted against
flares, smoke and
explosions during an
attack on Hamburg,
Germany, 1943.
IMPERIAL WAR MUSEUM,
C 3371

Crews were given a full briefing before they took off for each raid, with maps and details of the exact targets they were to hit. However, George remembers that the temptation to get out of the range of ground fire as fast as possible was sometimes greater than the desire for accuracy.

> They might brief us to go in at 15,000 feet – but we used to say, we'll get up to 20,000, because the higher you are the less chance of getting hit by ack-ack. Ack-ack was the danger, not the fighters. We dropped the bombs at 20,000, the maximum we could get up. If we could have got up to 30,000 we'd have flown up at 30,000! Oh no, the intelligence officers had got no control over us once we were up in the air. But we'd come back and the logbook would say we did our raid at 15,000.

> *Were there other planes, other crews flying higher than they were supposed to?*

> Oh, they all did – all the crews. It was always a case of survival. When we pushed the tit, dropped the bombs, it automatically dropped a photo flash

and took a photo of the area. In the photo they counted over 1000 flashes, that's anti-aircraft guns going off. Usually a lot of bombs are dropped before you get to the target, you let them go away and come home. Intelligence used to interrogate us – where we'd struck night fighters, where we'd struck anti-aircraft, the amount of anti-aircraft, and, 'Did you see the target? Did you drop your bombs on the target?' They wanted to know all these things. I used to say, 'Of course I dropped my bombs on the target.' And they'd come back with a photo, they took the film and told us how close to the target we were, 'You're so many thousand feet off.' I'd say to them, 'Looking through my bomb sight it was right on.' Of course if your plane is at an angle, the cross looks as if it's on the ground, but if the plane is, say, nose down a bit, well it throws the cross backwards. I said, 'With all the ack-ack, you couldn't keep the plane flying level when we took the photograph.'

Did you really care whether you hit the target or not?

No, not really. Just get rid of them and get back. I was thankful we got back. There's hundreds of aircrew killed, missing each raid.

I always remember the intelligence officer would give us a briefing and we were told, 'Don't forget, there's only one good German and that's a dead one.' They were very hard in their attitude. I felt sorry for the German people towards the end of it. They got bombed, gee . . . it wasn't necessary, I don't think. To bomb like Butcher Harris, he was in charge of bomber command, Air Commodore Harris, and he used to give the orders, 'Bomb Germany and bomb them to smithereens.' He used to say, 'There's only one good German and that's a dead one.'

We used to call the Ruhr Valley the Happy Valley. It was the industrial area of Germany, the Ruhr Valley. We used to bomb there quite often, and they had plenty of ack-ack guns. Because the Ruhr Valley is a series of cities, you can't help but hit the cities. We just bombed whole cities. They wanted to break the German population. The intelligence fellows used to say to us, 'If we break the population down, the war will stop, the Germans will throw in the towel.' It used to be, when we first started we'd go for the target. But later we'd bomb the whole city. You might bomb one quarter of Berlin and the next time you go back there, bomb the next area, until the city has been saturated with bombs. Oh it was a cruel war, cruel war.

Could you ever think about who the bombs were falling on?

Not really – my main aim was to drop the bombs, get out and get back to base.

In spite of attempts to stay out of the way of anti-aircraft fire, it was impossible to avoid it.

Well, we were hit every time. We used to go back in the daylight to where our plane was parked, and you could see all the holes in it and the tradesmen there, they used a drill and take the part off that had blown holes in it and they'd pop another part on. But you'd go back, have a yarn with the armourers and the flight mechanics and so forth.

I remember when we were doing a raid one time over Germany there was a hell of a scream coming over the intercom. Our rear gunner got hit by the flak and he was screaming out. And the engineer was a Welshman called Taffy. Taffy, he had to crawl back and drag him out of his turret and lay him out in the fuselage of the plane. That's all he could do. He was hit in the shoulders, just exploding shells. He survived, Maxi survived. Maxi McLauchlan, he came from Sydney. He was only off for about a couple of

Bombed-out buildings in Berlin, May 1945. IMPERIAL WAR MUSEUM, C 5284

months and he was back with us again. All our crew survived. Luck. Just plain luck. There was a lot of luck, and luck was on our side. I survived it. Our crew survived it.

I saw a crew bailing out once, and I saw the German ack-ack shooting at them. You could see the tracers going through their chutes.

Were they alive?

I don't know. You see the bodies on the end of the chute, that's all. I only saw three or four, but there are seven in the crew. It's hard to get out of a plane if it's twisting and diving into the ground. It was out of control and the crew had to abandon it. You just took it as part of the job, that's all. You just say, 'Oh, hard luck, mate.'

Because of the altitude at which they flew, bomber crews had special clothing to keep them warm.

I used to have an electric vest, electric pants to go on my uniform, and electric gloves. Oh they were warm. I wouldn't like to fly without them, you'd be frozen. I used to have a helmet, flying helmet and balaclava on top of that. I used to dress up for the cold. In wintertime, when you're 20,000 feet up it's minus 30 degrees, and you touch the metal with your bare hand it will take your skin off your hand – you've got to be very careful.

So this electrically heated clothing, where was it getting its power from?

From the batteries you plug into it. The motors used to charge the batteries up, each motor had two generators and that's how we boosted our power. That operated the gun turrets and all those things.

It was not only when he was flying that George struggled to keep warm. He remembers the winters at 514 Squadron's base at Waterbeach, near Cambridge.

I was living in a Nissan hut, you know it was like half a tank, concrete floor. They had a fire in there – you could light a fire and stoke it up with coal for heat. Oh, it was cold. I used to go to sleep in my bunk with my inner flying suit on to keep warm – it was like a kapok thing, lined with wool in the centre.

If we'd gone well into Germany on a raid they'd put a meal on for us when we got back. You'd go in there and you'd say the name of your crew, and I remember a Kiwi fellow, we used to call him Ten Egg Rogers, he used to take notice of all the crews that were missing. He used to go and order their egg rations too. Nine times out of ten they'd give it to him. I tell you I got sick of mashed potatoes and cheese. We used to get a lot of that. It wasn't flash food, but it was food. Of course everything was rationed.

I didn't smoke very much. What started me smoking . . . when we got back from a raid we were interviewed by the intelligence officer and on the table they had a bowl of Woodbine cigarettes, you could help yourself, and they had a cask of rum. You can put some rum in your coffee while you're waiting, while they're interviewing you. And then it was back to the old Nissan hut and go off to sleep. Have a shower and go down to the local village and go to the tavern and have a yarn with the people there.

On leave George sometimes got to London, and he has lasting memories of those visits.

I remember I was walking back to my hotel once when the Germans came over London and I went into a shopfront just to get shelter, not from the bombs but from the spent ack-ack shells from the British. They were raining down on the cobblestone street just like hailstones – you could see them bouncing in the street, down the roadway. They were small pieces,

George Wirepa and his crew from 514 Squadron, 1944. George is second from the right.
GEORGE WIREPA COLLECTION

but still you'd get a nasty hit if they hit you on the head or on the face. Later they had the flying bombs come over, and the first time I saw one I was with my friend Maxi, 'Look, look!' And then they stopped and they went straight down, they must have exploded a couple of blocks away, and the blast came right over the building and the next thing I picked myself up down the bottom of a ramp I was walking up. The blast blew us down there! We were alright – just cleaned ourselves up and went up again. Doodlebugs, we used to call them.

When D-Day dawned, in most respects it was just another day for George's crew.

They didn't tell us it was D-Day. But I remember the intelligence officer saying, 'There's to be no bombs ejected or jettisoned in the Channel. You have to bring your bombs out and take them out to the Wash and jettison them in the Wash.' He said, 'Any hang-up bombs getting stuck, don't drop them over the Channel', and he kept on saying that.

But I remember about five o'clock in the morning we were standing outside our plane waiting for our turn to get on board and start up the motors, and I saw all these planes going past. I said, 'Jeepers they're in close formation.' They were DC3s, Dakotas, and one of the crew said, 'They're not flying in formation, they're towing gliders.' And I said, 'Invasion!' Suddenly the penny dropped. He said, 'Yes, they're going over there and we'll get there before them' – because it's faster in the Lancaster.

Our target was German artillery. According to intelligence they were outside the town of Falaise, near a forest, these German artillery guns, and we had to bomb those so they couldn't fire on the boats going across the Channel. We dropped our bombs. We wiped the whole bloody forest out. Nothing but smoke coming up from the ground. And we were coming back, I saw all the craft – as far as we could see. We were about 8000 feet up and had a great sight, all these craft going over to France. All the barges going across, hundreds of barges. And ahead of them was the whole British navy there, firing guns around Falaise and round the landing area. I said to the crew, 'The invasion's on, mate.' I thought it was great. I knew the war wouldn't last for much longer.

I remember a bridge just south of Le Havre – the Germans had mined the bridge, according to intelligence, and we went and bombed it and so the troops had to go on barges across this river. This was on D-Day too. It was the first time we did two bombing raids in one day. The first wave

George Wirepa, 2004. ALISON PARR

in, they blew the thing to bits but we just dropped our bombs. On D-Day, all the planes, American planes, fighter planes, twin-engine bombers, the whole works, the whole sky was covered with Allied aircraft, and we were part of it. I've never seen so many planes in the air in one hit.

At the beginning of 1945, George was promoted in rank to flying officer and completed a tour of 30 raids with 514 Squadron. Later that year he returned home and became a builder, working for Fletchers. In Gisborne in 1960 he met Betty Jones, who was to be his partner for 40 years.

George's wartime years are now 'just a sad memory'. He dwells on the bombing raids he was part of and remains unhappy about some of the orders received from Bomber Command.

I forget the name of this place we bombed in Germany, it was a city in the east. But it was murder. Straight-out murder. It was not necessary to bomb that city. Bomber Harris just wanted to impress the Russians with the might of the RAF, that's all he wanted to do. It was daylight when we dropped our bombs. We could see and there was no ack-ack there, no resistance, no nothing. We were told to bomb the whole city. I felt disgusted. I thought, what's wrong? I didn't feel happy. No. The Brits should know what it was like, they'd been through the air raids with the Luftwaffe over London.

Eric Krull, 1945. ERIC KRULL COLLECTION

Eric Krull

LIEUTENANT, LCT 708, RN

You know, when I saw the shambles on D-Day I thought, my God, we probably have had it. But it wasn't so.

WHEN WAR WAS DECLARED IN 1939, EIGHTEEN-YEAR-OLD ERIC KRULL WAS working on his family's farm in Manawatu and thinking of going to 'the Argentine' with a friend. He got the adventure he wished for – but not in South America. In 1941 he was accepted into the Royal Navy's Scheme B to train as an officer, and later set sail for the United Kingdom. After arriving in Portsmouth in May 1942 he was soon despatched to destroyers to spend the next few months in training – hunting submarines in the North Sea in HMS *Echo* and HMS *Obdurate*.

Eric's father had served with the New Zealand Rough Riders in the South African War. His grandfather, Frederick Augustus Krull, had emigrated to New Zealand from Germany in the 1850s, becoming German consul in his adopted country. Eric's German origins were never a real hindrance in the Royal Navy.

> When I was training as a matelot, one of the British – he'd been in the navy donkey's years, a warrant officer, a really hard nut – said, 'German bastard, eh?' But he wasn't too serious about it. I didn't take any offence. I just grinned at him.

In 1943, at the age of 23, Eric became a commissioned officer – a sub-lieutenant – after training at King Alfred College in Hove. It was well known that the Royal Navy would play a crucial role in the anticipated invasion of France, and Eric and his skipper, Dick Offer, were soon assigned to their ship – Landing Craft Tanks (LCT) 708.

At Lowestoft we picked up ours. In the shipyard it was just a mess. They were making these landing craft, and it was just a mass of bits of steel and grubbiness all round and we had to commission it, as they say – so we had to clean it up. It was about the length of this house, a couple of hundred feet. It took half a dozen tanks and quite a lot of miscellaneous stuff. It had accommodation for we two officers. We had a bunk each and a washbasin. The bridge was just above us. As ships they were slow and flat-bottomed, mass-produced. Without a load they took every wave and were uncomfortable – thump, thump, thump.

I was the second officer. Dick Offer was first officer and he was about 35, very experienced, and we were going to be despatched early, they wanted experienced men. He was from London. He represented Britain at rowing in the Empire Games and was a veteran sailor.

LCT 708 was crewed by a dozen young men. When the skipper and his second officer met them, they were taken aback.

Because we'd been brought up and been trained as officers, we obeyed all the rules and we were all properly dressed and everything had to be spot on. When the crew arrived I thought, hell, what have we got here? They were all dressed up in all sorts of clothing. They must have been posted from various places like Portsmouth, naval bases. English, Scots, Irish, hard cases. They were seamen, twenty or 21 at the most, conscripted probably.

Well, I told them to get cracking and I couldn't believe that they didn't take too much notice of me! However, we finally got around to some sort of an understanding, but they were a hard-case lot. But, you know, they came from very poor families and we can't really understand the conditions that they lived in in their home life.

For nearly twelve months, the crew of LCT 708 trained in landing their vessel on beaches.

We must have sailed round most of England and been to all sorts of places. Maybe a little place like Instow or Bideford where there was always a senior naval officer, probably a retired senior officer. They used to rather enjoy coming out with us and we would give them plenty of beer, and I think they'd all been used to fairly heavy drinking and they'd come out to enjoy themselves.

And what about the crew? Did the crew get their rum rations?

> We had to keep the key strictly under control. It was a terrible sin if the key was lost. We had to keep the rum locker key in the safe which contained all our confidential papers – where we were to go, the numbers of our boats and all the details.

Secrecy shrouded specific details of the landing in France, but everyone knew it was imminent. In Southampton and its surrounds there were miles of military vehicles gathering. By D-Day there were 4000 ships in the Channel.

> All flotillas were tied up in trots, as they call them, side by side all along the wharves of Southampton. The King and Queen sailed up shortly before D-Day to farewell us and wave to us. The royal barge sailed as close to us as possible.

Even though both officers and crew knew they were heading for an assault on the French coast, Eric can't recall any combined operations training with the army. Surprisingly, when they loaded up at the beginning of June, it was the first time the vessel had carried vehicles. D-Day would be the first time it had landed tanks and men.

Their destination was Gold Beach. On board for the invasion, alongside six Sherman tanks, were four self-propelled artillery, small vehicles carrying 4-inch guns. There was also a jeep and an ambulance. In all, about twenty army personnel, including a doctor and two officers, were waiting for the order to sail.

When bad weather meant D-Day was postponed for 24 hours, thousands of men had to stay on board their vessels and wait. Eric remembers that the tank and gun crews on LCT 708 were edgy during the delay – and they drank.

> I can't remember where they got all the grog from, but they got pretty full. Some of them fell overboard and we had to rescue them. We were tied up in the Solent, further down at this stage ready to go, and there was an 11-knot tide there, it was like a rushing river and made manoeuvring difficult. These fellows were tripping all over the place. Of course they got very seasick crossing the Channel, poor devils.

On the morning of 6 June orders were finally given for the fleet to head for Normandy. Eric felt relief and apprehension.

Troops and vehicles on board a landing craft head for the Normandy coast, D-Day, 1944.

It was a tremendous decision Eisenhower had to make. I didn't envy him at all, because it was still very rough when we sailed. It was borderline as to whether we could make it across the Channel or not and land on the beaches. I thought, hell! This is going to be big.

Were you scared?

Surprisingly, no. When you're young you don't think of possible danger, but I suppose you have the feeling, well nothing can happen to me. And strangely you don't feel much fear.

What was the atmosphere like going over?

Quiet, very quiet, because a lot of them were sick. The skipper and I were both up on the bridge and the army was down below on the tank deck and in their vehicles, and we didn't hear from them.

The officer in charge of the army personnel on board was Captain Tony Gregson. He had a nineteen-year-old South African second lieutenant. In the two days before sailing, Eric and Tony became good friends.

I thoroughly enjoyed it. I had a lot of time for Tony. One of those typical Englishmen, very brave. Fair haired, rather delicate-looking fellow really, but he was an extremely nice person.

We were assigned to make the landing an hour before the main assault, so we had to form a beachhead if we could, to set the structure so that other craft could come in. We were half an hour late because of the roughness of the sea. We arrived at zero half instead of zero one. We made a first attempt and lowered the door, and we thought we were on the beach but we weren't on the beach, and a couple of Sherman tanks went off and they sank. They had snorkels which were supposed to carry them through a certain depth of water, but it was just too deep.

And they were tanks with crew?

Yes, and they were drowned, of course. And then we kedged further offshore and the skipper, Dick Offer, said, 'Well, there's only one way we're going to do it and that's to go full speed ahead and see what happens.' So having pulled further off the beach we ploughed into all these obstructions, and it was then that all the chaos started because – we weren't actually under fire at this stage, there was a rocket ship beside us and this was cradles of rockets all aimed at Caen – but the 88-millimetre from pillboxes shooting at us landed a shell in the rocket ship and the thing just disappeared. We just didn't see it. The whole rocket ship went up. It disappeared. There was just one huge explosion and it was gone.

And the crew?

Disappeared. Don't know what happened to them. I didn't see. They must have been blown to bits. There was a lot of debris. Bits of metal, wood, objects from the wheelhouse. Mainly bits of steel, I suppose, chunks of steel and wooden debris. We couldn't take much notice, we were too involved ourselves. We made a full-speed-ahead charge at the beach and almost made it, but we couldn't get quite on. There was a depth of water to go through and the sea was very rough, and it was then that one of the mines, Teller mines they called them, they were underwater mines, exploded.

I suppose the craft was wider than this room and there were two winch-houses, one on each side, and I was in one winch-house and Tony was in the other. I suppose we were only a couple of metres apart, and I suddenly saw him disappear with this underwater explosion which left a gaping hole in the deck and took some of the superstructure – he just went up in the air and came down with one side shattered. He just landed on the deck and I thought, oh my God. He was a mess.

We had what's called the Neil Robertson stretcher, which wraps around and keeps him horizontal. We had a lot of morphine aboard and I used it all on him and thought, if he dies . . . I rather hope he does, because he was terribly wounded. I put myself in his position and thought, well, what have I got left? He just kept saying, 'I'm cold, Kiwi.' I said, 'Is there anything . . . what else can I do?' – 'I'm just cold.'

Do you think he realised how badly he was injured?

I don't know that he did. But I thought if we can get him back . . . so I signalled the destroyer, send a boat to collect a wounded officer, and of course that's not done in the navy. You're supposed to request it very carefully, and I got such a tick-off for not going through the right procedure.

I thought, this has got to be extraordinarily painful, and the best thing I can do is try and ease it for him. He's got to be hoisted into a boat in the Neil Robertson stretcher and then hoisted back on board the destroyer. And so I tried to imagine if I was in that position, I wouldn't want to feel anything if I could help it. I just had these tubes of morphine, like a tube of toothpaste – gooey stuff, needle on the end. I think I put the needle on and just squeezed it. I think I used two or three. No first-aid training at all. Any problems, just give it to them, to whoever was in trouble. Anyway, they did send a boat over and collected him, and miraculously the doctor on board was Tony's best mate. Tony lived, apparently. I believe he was paralysed all down one side.

And then we were crashing up and down in the water and these small landing craft were lowered from the ships about a mile offshore and they were coming in in waves. And as we would rise on a wave they would get washed underneath, and we would come down on top of them, and we killed dozens of them, these landing-craft crew, because the sea was still very rough and they were just getting bashed against us and under us.

The doctor, he tried to get ashore in the jeep and couldn't make it. It was being tossed about for a while. The driver was sitting on the hood, screaming his head off. He was just screaming out, 'Help me! Help me!' . . . Poor beggar.

What happened to the doctor?

Well, he drowned. I don't know quite what happened, but our coxswain said, 'Oh, I'll rescue them.' So we tied a rope around him, and he was a pretty good swimmer and he swam over, but another mine went off fairly close and concussed our coxswain. So we had to haul him aboard quickly. We didn't really know what happened – it was all getting pretty messy by this stage. The driver and doctor were both lost.

Then this 88-millimetre shore battery decided that it was our turn. I could see this splash coming towards us and then finally they put a shell through us. I think two shells hit us. They went just above the water level, and one came down the side and ruined all our food supply. A Royal Navy cruiser laying offshore was our saviour – its guns destroyed the pillbox, landed a shell right into it and killed all the inmates. We were spared. And from there on we were pretty safe.

If Tony Gregson, the army officer, was so badly wounded, who was dealing with the rest of the army crew that were trying to get on shore?

The little South African, and he was terribly upset. He'd burst into tears and he said, 'I don't know what to do.' The skipper was busy with the ship, so I had to advise him as best I could and said, 'Well, the main thing is to get them ashore and then try and collect them up.' In the distance we could see a Union Jack. It had been hoisted on a pole on the top of a sandhill. All I could do was to say, 'Just gather them and you can get them ashore now, it's pretty safe to get them ashore. And when you've got them there, take them up to the flag and hope that there are a lot of others there in the same boat.'

An aerial view, shot by Allied Intelligence, of part of the Gold Beach area, Normandy, D-Day, 1944. IMPERIAL WAR MUSEUM, MH 24887

The young South African officer set off – and that was the last Eric heard of him. The door of the landing craft was down by this stage, and some vehicles were able to unload.

> Maybe a couple got ashore safely and I think the self-propelled artillery, they mainly got ashore alright. They were firing as we went in. They were supposed to be also aimed at Caen, which was the town nearby. I don't think they really knew what they were doing but they were just letting them off, hoping. But how they could imagine they could fire accurately

One of the invasion beaches in Normandy, the day after D-Day. Landing craft and barrage balloons can be seen in the distance. IMPERIAL WAR MUSEUM, A 23947

while we were dancing about so much, I don't know. Still, that was their order, so they did it.

As you looked up the beach, it was a mess. There were stranded craft and all sorts of little craft, big craft, a hell of a mess really. But we didn't know anything about the others much, because we were all on our own and had to look after ourselves. There was no method of getting in touch or walking along to see how they were, or anything like that. I thought it was hopeless. I thought we'd never make it. I thought, you know, this is a failure. We just kept doing what we could, and we thought we were extremely lucky to be on the boat and not going ashore. That's what we secretly thought.

What was your opinion of those who did make it onto the shore, who got there?

Well they were just ordinary soldiers. They weren't complaining – they hardly said a word. They just got their orders to go, and they were pretty tense I think then. Those manning the self-propelled artillery and the tanks – we couldn't see them. They were locked up in their tanks. I think the ambulance got ashore alright in the end, because it was the last off. But of course the doctor died and they only had the driver. I don't know how far that ambulance could have gone in the sand. I can't remember what sort of traction it had. I don't think it had any proper tracks.

Eric also remembers how noisy Gold Beach was that day with the sound of vehicles, guns and shouting. Along the shore he reckons there were 50 or 60 craft, each of which would have been carrying about twenty men. Some of the soldiers who were making it to the beach were wounded. And in the water around them, as well as the floating debris from destroyed boats, there were also bodies.

Even before the chaos of the landing, Eric had been aware that he was playing a role in an historic event.

I thought this was it, or not. I thought if it fails we've had it. When I saw the shambles on D-Day I thought, my God, we probably have had it. But it wasn't so.

How long did all of that take?

Oh it took most of the day, and the tide went out. We had to wait for the tide again, and we pulled off and had instructions to get back to England as quickly as we could, and get repaired and get back into service again. So we went back to Tilbury docks.

During the melee on Gold Beach, Eric himself had received some minor wounds. Shrapnel had gone through his hand and he had a bashed knee that troubles him still. He and the crew of LCT 708 had a short leave while the boat was repaired, and then they continued making trips across the Channel, with Glen Miller music on the radio for the benefit of the American troops they were transporting, mainly to Gold Beach.

We'd land them on the beach and the tide would go out so we'd have a whole day to spend there. In the summer we'd swim and other days I used to enjoy walking. I'd walk all day into France. I enjoyed what I saw. Wish I could have gone further – I'd just follow any way that I could find, and in those days I knew enough French to make myself understood, and sometimes I'd be asked in by a family to have some bread and cheese, which I did and they didn't know where Nouvelle-Zélande was.

They didn't like the Americans. I remember standing outside a gate one day and a truck-load of Americans went past and were flinging cigarettes out to the French people, and they didn't like it. The Americans probably thought it was kindness; the French thought it was arrogance.

Occasionally the landing craft brought back German prisoners from France – about twenty or thirty at a time.

Eric Krull's LCT 708 taking part in the celebrations in Bideford on VE Day, 1945. He remembers, 'We were going backwards and forwards up the river, taking these kids for rides all day, and there were flags flying. There was great excitement.' MARY CLEAVER COLLECTION

Eric Krull, 2004. ALISON PARR

Young, poor souls, simple souls, scared stiff, happy to be captured I think. Very inexperienced. I'd say they'd be barely twenty. They were just giggling and laughing among themselves and looking around, bewildered.

When the news came that the war in Europe had been won Eric was in Bideford, in Devon. The naval commander put on a big party in a hotel. On VE Day the festivities continued.

There was a celebration and a march-past in Bideford. This was opposite the Bideford Hotel and the commander said, 'Well, I'm having you up on the dais to represent New Zealand.' So I was up there with the mayor and the commander and the dignitaries, and I had a great time that day. I felt great – they saluted as they went past.

When he returned to New Zealand, Eric Krull went back to the family farm, which he managed until his retirement. In 1948 he married Noemi Craine.

On reflection, he believes his war service taught him worthwhile lessons.

Better than a university education. Knowledge of the world, people, different sorts of people, how to handle people, how to treat them – just a general knowledge, I suppose. You learnt so much, really.

What are your thoughts about war now, and its place in human life?

It's absolutely stupid. It's cruel. It's horrible, and I just cannot understand why people cannot learn that nobody wins. So many of the best people have been killed . . . a lot of our best young men who would have led the country.

Trevor Mullinder, 1944. TREVOR MULLINDER COLLECTION

Trevor Mullinder

FLYING OFFICER, 487 (NZ) SQUADRON, FIGHTER COMMAND, RAF

*We knew the big show was coming. . . . This time, success was
absolutely important.*

Three of Trevor Mullinder's uncles had fought in the first world
War. His grandmother was a German refugee, so her sons had gone to fight
against her motherland. A generation later, Trevor also went to fight his grandmother's people. Born in Taihape in 1919, Trevor went from Hastings Boys' High
School to Wellington Teachers' College, where he was when war was declared.
He disliked the idea of direct combat and chose the air force as a more impersonal
form of warfare.

After some training with the RNZAF in New Zealand he went to Canada to
the Empire Air Training School, and was commissioned there before leaving for
England at the end of 1942. At Gravesend, Kent, Trevor joined 487 (NZ) Squadron
as a navigator, flying Mosquitos – very fast fighter-bombers. He teamed up with
Pilot Officer Gerry Whincop from Wellington. The squadron was engaged in
bombing and 'intruder' raids into France at night, covering night fighter aerodromes while Allied 'heavies' went on to bomb targets in Germany.

About a month before D-Day they began practising low-level attacks on strategic targets such as railway lines, ammunition dumps and transport vehicles. Just
days before 6 June the squadron received its instructions for the invasion – to attack
roads and rail junctions. Trevor remembers the tension after that briefing.

> I was a sprog on the job, Gerry and I were, but we repaired to the various
> rooms that we had to gather the information, and some of the hard-
> bitten NCOs who'd been through the mill, you could see them, they got

RAF ground crew update the record of a New Zealand Mosquito bomber. WAR HISTORY
COLLECTION, ALEXANDER TURNBULL LIBRARY, 1/4-018334-F

the twitch. Some of these boys had been just normal Kiwi kids, and when
they realised that this was the big show, it just hit 'em – this is it. Because
we all knew that the Second Front was an absolute essential. We knew
the big show was coming and it's like a big football match, you're all
keyed up for it. Great to be part of a team. I think we were more nervous
because it was a much bigger thing. This time, success was absolutely
important.

At two o'clock on the morning of D-Day, Trevor and Gerry set off for their target
in Normandy – the city of Alençon.

It was a junction of roads about 30 miles inland. The attack was to stop any
traffic, any military movement up to confront the blokes on the beach.
Very important, actually.

He and Gerry successfully bombed their target. On their way back to England, about twenty miles off the French coast, they flew past the glider train carrying thousands of paratroops into enemy territory. It took about two minutes for them to pass all the gliders.

> We were flying about 300 miles an hour. The glider train was huge. There were hundreds of them. It was so dark they had their lights on. They put them on then to avoid collision. Of course, when they got to within five miles of the enemy coast they'd ditch all lights. Those fellas had a pretty tough job because their timing had to be absolutely perfect. I felt sorry for them in a way because we knew that the slaughter of the German paratroopers was terrific, and I thought of the casualties in Crete.
>
> I've got no real conception, but looking at that glider train, it must have stretched between 60 and 80 miles across. We were right over the top of them. It must have been miles deep. Then underneath them in the Channel was the invasion fleet – thousands of ships, they seemed very close together, stirring the sea almost white with their wakes – a marvellous sight.

Were you prepared for that sight?

No, no. Didn't have an inkling of the immensity of the thing. We didn't. It's only afterwards. I never had an idea of the effort that had gone in to prepare for everything that took place.

Five days after D-Day, Trevor received devastating news – his brother Theo had died of wounds near Cassino in Italy. Although he was given the option of being taken off duty, Trevor chose to keep flying and that night set off for another operation over France.

He and Gerry completed their attack successfully and were returning to England when they were attacked by another Mosquito.

> I'd just given Gerry a new course, and then the attack came in. I got hit in the leg, just the calf, about half an inch from the bone, went straight through. Bled a bit, but I was too occupied with doing what I had to do. I lost the heel of my flying boot and the instrument panel was shattered. There was a lot of noise, squealing metal. I don't know how many times Gerry went round, because he couldn't control the plane. It must have

The telegram Trevor's parents received just before he was shot down, confirming the death of his brother in Italy. Telegrams like this were the means by which thousands of New Zealand families learnt about the death of sons, husbands and brothers during the war. TREVOR MULLINDER COLLECTION

been something jammed in the tailplane. He decided in that time that he couldn't manage the plane, and that's when he said, 'Out!', 'cos we had difficulty talking with each other in the noise. So I went through all the things I had to do.

The preparation for abandoning the plane included destroying a black box containing operational information, and eating the code of the day, written on rice paper.

Then I took off my flak helmet and my flak suit and I picked my parachute up off the floor and jettisoned the door. I got the nod from Gerry. I got out of my seat, clamped the parachute to my chest, got to the door, and my last sight of Gerry was when I looked around to see how he was getting on, and I must have leaned forward a bit, because the next thing I was just sucked out of the aircraft. I was lucky I didn't have my hand on the ripcord

Trevor's membership certificate for the Caterpillar Club, awarded to those who had jumped to safety with the aid of a parachute. TREVOR MULLINDER COLLECTION

because it most likely would have pulled straight away. I waited until I saw the tailplane go over and then I pulled. I had to pull straight away, before I reached a terminal velocity, because I didn't know how close to the earth we were, and that's when the chute opened with a terrific bang and really whacked me between the legs. It incapacitated me for quite a while.

It was a very boisterous night, a windy night. I didn't know where I was in relation to the earth, and the first thing I knew that the earth was anywhere near was when I hit it. You see, it was pitch-black.

He can remember his thoughts in the two or three minutes he reckons it took him to reach the earth.

I thought of my parents, that was the first thing. I knew just after Theo going like that how upset they would be, and I think that was possibly when I hit the deck. It seems a bit dramatic, but that's just exactly how it

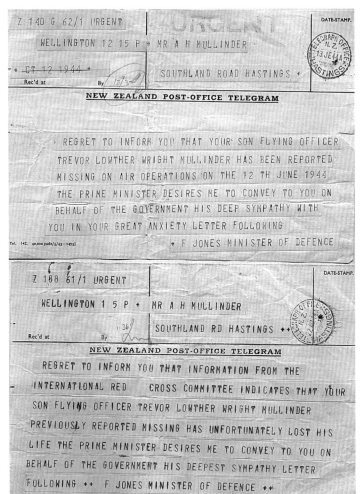

Z 140 G 62/1 URGENT · URGENT · DATE-STAMP.

WELLINGTON 12 15 P + MR A H MULLINDER

+ CT 12 1944 + SOUTHLAND ROAD HASTINGS +
Rec'd at ___ By ___

NEW ZEALAND POST-OFFICE TELEGRAM

· REGRET TO INFORM YOU THAT YOUR SON FLYING OFFICER
TREVOR LOWTHER WRIGHT MULLINDER HAS BEEN REPORTED
MISSING ON AIR OPERATIONS ON THE 12 TH JUNE 1944
THE PRIME MINISTER DESIRES ME TO CONVEY TO YOU ON
BEHALF OF THE GOVERNMENT HIS DEEP SYMPATHY WITH
YOU IN YOUR GREAT ANXIETY LETTER FOLLOWING
+ F JONES MINISTER OF DEFENCE

Z 188 61/1 URGENT · DATE-STAMP.

WELLINGTON 1 5 P + MR A H MULLINDER

SOUTHLAND RD HASTINGS ++
Rec'd at ___ By ___

NEW ZEALAND POST-OFFICE TELEGRAM

REGRET TO INFORM YOU THAT INFORMATION FROM THE
INTERNATIONAL RED CROSS COMMITTEE INDICATES THAT YOUR
SON FLYING OFFICER TREVOR LOWTHER WRIGHT MULLINDER
PREVIOUSLY REPORTED MISSING HAS UNFORTUNATELY LOST HIS
LIFE THE PRIME MINISTER DESIRES ME TO CONVEY TO YOU ON
BEHALF OF THE GOVERNMENT HIS DEEPEST SYMPATHY LETTER
FOLLOWING ++ F JONES MINISTER OF DEFENCE ++

Official telegrams received by Trevor's parents in New Zealand reveal that he was right to worry about the news his parents may hear after he was shot down. The office of New Zealand's Minister of Defence misinformed them that Trevor had been killed. It was three months before they received a letter telling them he was, in fact, safe in a POW camp in Germany. Because of delays in wartime communications, it was common for such news to be staggered, resulting in an emotional roller-coaster for families. TREVOR MULLINDER COLLECTION

happened. When I hit the deck the wind got the canopy and I was dragged, and it took me quite a while to gather the shroud or canopy in so I wouldn't get dragged. I still had my Mae West [life jacket] that I had to get off me, and then I set about going towards a clump of trees, or something dark, that I could see. I wanted to hide.

As I started to walk, with arms full of chute and Mae West, I felt the squelching in my flying boot, so I thought well, no sense in bleeding to death if you've survived a parachute jump – I'd better stop and see what I can do. We always flew with an escape kit. But I found I couldn't see anything, so I had to get my torch, which was a red light, out of my Mae

West, and I was sitting in the middle of a paddock. When I looked at it the next day it was silly, because I shouldn't have been drawing attention to the fact that I was there at all. But anyway, it had stopped bleeding, it was just gathering in the sole of the boot. It looked a lot worse then. In daylight there was a big hole where the flak came out and a little hole where it went in.

Were you in any pain?

No. No pain – I was too keyed up with everything else. It was painful a couple of days after, 'cos it swelled up around the puncture.

I went into this little forest, a glade I suppose you'd call it, and I got down in the best place I could find and wrapped myself up in the chute and – I might have gone to sleep, I doubt it – but in daylight I was pretty wide awake and I heard a person moving in the bush. Then I heard a voice, 'Monsieur'. I didn't answer, and it got closer and closer and, 'Monsieur'. And then I saw him, a French boy, about sixteen years old, and they were looking for me. He said, in his own language, 'Get out of here, the Germans during the day like coming here to hide from the aircraft that are bombing them.' So he took me into this barn and we pulled these bales of hay out and made a good sleeping place, put my parachute in there and that was that. Left me there.

Well, later on that day I had to relieve myself. So I got out and I looked outside the barn, and there were bloody Huns everywhere. I couldn't move – so I relieved myself, and went back and stayed till dark. The boy brought me a bottle of water and something to eat, not very much – bread, something like scone. And until the next day I just stayed stuck. But every time I had to relieve myself I'd have a look round and it was a no-go. I think if I'd moved at night-time I would have walked into them.

What could you see from the barn?

Only one house. And I think it was the mayor of the village – I think the name was Bosbanard, because I asked the boy. The old man from the house brought me a bottle of cognac, and I thought, oh good, he's going to give me a drink. And he made me roll up my pants leg and he saw what it was and he poured a damn good brew of cognac on my leg. Of course he was right, I suppose, but oh hell! I thought that was a waste of good drink. It hurt, too. God, it bites! But it certainly fixed the leg.

Trevor stayed like this for six or seven days. The boy kept coming, sometimes during the day, to give him cheese and bread. Trevor's escape kit had a chocolate 'D bar' which he rationed, along with a tube of condensed milk. He soon began to suffer hay fever from the straw he was lying on. To keep the pollen from his nose and muffle the noise from his sneezing, he cut up some silk from his parachute for a handkerchief. In spite of his best efforts, Trevor was eventually captured. A young German armed with a gun found him in the barn – and Trevor's German origins confronted him.

> He was only a kid, taking all his time to be sixteen, seventeen, maybe eighteen. He was shaking so much, and when I looked at him carefully, he was the dead spit of my brother when he was that age, blonde, blue-eyed. Of course I was conscious of my brother at the time – it struck me. He was the only German I ever saw that did look like my brother. I was the first enemy he had ever seen, most likely, and he certainly was the first one I'd ever seen. I wasn't shaking. I'd more or less accepted the fact that my cake was pretty near dough.

That evening Trevor was taken to a cave in a hillside where he was left for the next two or three days without food. He was given only water.

> You see, this is the old idea of softening up for interrogation. Psychologically it's sound – if you're in starvation or are anxious, you're likely to give yourself away, even unexpectedly. So we more or less expected that kind of treatment.
>
> In the cave I met one badly burned American officer, a pilot, and another young fellow who wasn't burned. One was a bomber pilot and one was a fighter pilot. We were stacked into this cave with a barbed-wire sort of door to keep us in. I don't know whether the wounded American lived or died. He was unconscious most of the time and we couldn't make the guards realise. Finally we did get a doctor and he had a look at him, and I don't know what he said, but it wasn't very long afterwards that they took him away.

From the cave Trevor and the remaining American pilot were taken on another journey of about 65 kilometres.

> We got strafed on the way and we weren't allowed to get out of the vehicle. We were kept on the vehicle, a lorry, open top. And the guards

got into the ditches on the side of the road – and they indicated that if we made a break to get out, they would shoot. And of course we had to bear the brunt of being machine-gunned by our own aircraft. They came right down. That was the worst part about it, because we had done that, and we know what they do. They point the nose behind the target and they just pull the nose up and you can see the bullets going off the road and then through the target.

Did you say anything to each other?

Well, if you're about to be bloody well killed, or shot by the people in the ditch if you stay there when a machine gun spits out 1200 rounds per minute, you don't palaver very much. When you get stuck like that you try and scratch and claw your way out. You just want to get out. That's all I can remember of it. It's a terrible feeling. I've been bombed, but you can see the bomb fall in daylight, and if it's not a direct hit you've got a reasonable hope of avoiding it. But .5 bullets – these were Lightning aircraft that struck us – they make a helluva mess. They were American planes. But everything missed. They missed the truck completely. One of those bloody things that happens. You're either lucky, or you're unlucky.

By train and cattle truck, Trevor was then transported with about 50 or 60 other airmen to Dulag Luft at Oberursel, near Frankfurt in Germany, the main interrogation centre for captured Allied aircrew. Because Trevor had been attacked by friendly fire, there was no record of his plane going down and the Germans suspected he might be a saboteur.

At Dulag Luft he was put in a cell by himself for 27 days. He was kept in the small room with a narrow board bed, a small table, a blanket and a barred window and was allowed to go to the toilet once a day. Over several days he was subjected to the 'heat treatment', as he calls it. The temperature in the room was alternately made extremely hot and then cold, making sleeping difficult. He was interrogated several times, but refused to give more than his name and number. At one point, he was strip-searched.

I was carted off to the hospital for a strip search, and this is where the embarrassing part about it was. I had been on the run, starved, not washed for about four weeks by now, so they made me strip, get on the table, and a fairly young nursing sister intimated that she was going to do an internal search because they thought I might have had something there – and she went about it. And that, I suppose was the worst of the lot, 'cos I lost my tongue there. I told her, 'Now I know who's winning and losing this war when old German fraus have got to get their sexual kicks by poking around in the asses of captured airmen'. And oh, she understood me. The German guard pushed me on the bed, and I didn't catch what she said, she spoke only in German, but she started the same investigation again, but a bit rougher. You've got a sphincter nerve in the muscle there, and she pinched that and that's a hellish painful thing. It was unexpected too. I got such a shock, I yelled. And she spouted something in German, but it didn't mean anything to me. I was carted back off to the interrogator, and he was on the phone when I got in, and he ended up laughing. I didn't cotton on, but she had obviously said something and was ringing up because she did something she shouldn't have done, and he was laughing. He said to me, 'You haven't improved – I'm fed up with you, I make my recommendations, you'll hear about them.'

Airmen interrogated at Dulag Luft had a great fear of being passed on to the Gestapo. Trevor had other anxieties too. Throughout this period of imprisonment and interrogation he was worried about his parents and the likelihood they would think that he, like his brother, had been killed. His interrogator played on this fear and tried to persuade him that if he talked, the Red Cross would be informed and his parents could be told he was alive and well. But Trevor remained staunch and silent.

I felt in a bloody-minded state, I think. I was getting . . . I wasn't feeling in a weakened state, I think they just aroused a little bit of anger.

Eventually he was believed and sent by train under guard to Berlin and then to Stalag Luft 1, a POW camp in Barth, on the Baltic coast. To reach Berlin, he travelled with about 40 other men in a cattle wagon. For five days there was standing room only.

You slept where you were. You more or less took turns at lying down. You'd pair yourself off. I don't think we had any food until we got to Berlin, and then we had bugger all. But you see German transport was all to hell. It was the number one target.

Between the station at Barth and Stalag Luft 1 the men passed a group of prisoners from a nearby concentration camp.

An identification photo of Trevor taken in Stalag Luft 1, 1944. Trevor kept smiling deliberately because this irritated the German officer taking the shot. TREVOR MULLINDER COLLECTION

We had to march, and on our way to the prison we met a whole column of women, dressed in, well, concentration camp garb, and they were being marshalled along by German female guards. And there was not a smile. There must have been a couple of hundred. We thought it mighty strange, but at that time I don't think any of us believed that the Germans were really carrying out the extermination of Jews, or slave labour. I frankly didn't believe it myself, and thinking back it was only after the war when I went into one of those work places and saw and smelt the rotten kind of life that they were forced to lead before they were just butchered that I believed it.

Trevor arrived in Stalag Luft 1 in August 1944.

Very primitive – it was terribly overcrowded. We had a small room and we had, sometimes, 24 people in it. Dysentery was a shocker, really. And that's cruel. You'd see a fellow on the playing field – he'd be walking and then he'd break into a gallop and be running in the direction of the ablutions, and halfway you'd see him and he'd walk, he knew he was too late, there was not much you could do about that. A couple of them got it so bad, they died.

What sort of food did you have?

Oh gruel, but when I first got in the POW camp they had Red Cross rations, and you're supposed to get one of those a week. Well, we never did. I don't know what the Germans did with them, but they were pretty callous towards the end of the war. Food was very poor. I went down to below, I think it was 60 kilos – that's 120 pounds, I should have been round 150 to 160. I'm five eight and a half.

As a long-established prisoner of war camp, Stalag Luft 1 had a good library with books in English. Trevor spent a lot of his time reading. There was also the opportunity to burn off any frustrations.

When you had energy you played football – rugby. It was the most dicey, dangerous football I think we've ever played, because these blokes had been penned up, sure they were starved but they were pent up. There was no outlet for their feelings, no outlet for their sex drive, and they were really tough. To go down on the ball was almost like getting kicked to death, and if anybody got hurt there was no compassion from the sidelines, just screaming, 'Hang him on the wire! Hang him on the wire!' But it was good football, very competitive. We had English, Welsh, South African and New Zealand teams.

In April 1945, as liberation approached, the POWs remained fearful. There were rumours that the SS would kill all aircrew prisoners to encourage the German people to fight to the bitter end. The prisoners planned to defend themselves.

The German civilians hated our guts – we were airmen, we were the only ones that really brought the war home to the German population, and in a nasty way. So we were organised into shock battalions or brigades inside the POW camp. I, for example, found out how to kill

A newspaper produced by inmates of Stalag Luft 1 at the time of their liberation.
TREVOR MULLINDER COLLECTION

people in unarmed combat. We had paratroopers to teach us. We had good anti-intelligence. So when the Germans took to their scrapers my particular brigade was to go out onto the airfield and debomb it, get rid of all the booby traps and do everything to make the airfield serviceable so our heavies could land.

On the way to the airfield we came down a little sort of hollow in the ground, and I'm telling you this because you'll see how the climate at the end of the war affected the Germans. We found there was a little group, two women and a child in a pram. The women had been killed and the little fellow in the pram had a bullet hole right through his head. Now it wasn't the Russians, the Russians were nowhere near. We don't know whether it was the Germans, guilty Germans perhaps, that decided that what they'd done in Russia would be handed out to their own women, so they killed them and then took to their scrapers. We don't know. But that's the climate that was there. Really shocking. Unbelievable.

There were other horrors to confront, too. For three years a concentration camp had existed near Stalag Luft 1. A sub-camp of Ravensbruck, it housed 7000 women and men from 21 countries. It is likely that among them were the lines of women the POWs had passed as they arrived at Stalag Luft 1. Many of the prisoners were slave workers in the Heinkel aircraft factory beside the airfield where Trevor and the other POWs waited for Allied planes to pick them up. Hundreds of the concentration camp prisoners had died of hunger there, or been shot.

We were free to roam, and we saw the conditions where they'd put human beings – absolutely unbelievable stench, sickness, excrement, and these people were forced to live and die like this. Obviously a lot of people died there. From the mess in certain parts of the buildings it must have been a very cruel experience.

In the Heinkel works they were building the fuselages for the V2s, and sometimes we could see these terrific rockets going up in the air, but we didn't know what a V2 was because we were POWs and they weren't thought of when a lot of those POWs were captured. They were test-flying them maybe 50 to 100 miles from us, but when they got up in the air we could see the trail left behind.

So was it Jewish people who were working in that factory?

They were certainly Jewish, but there were possibly other German citizens there who were persona non grata to the Reich.

And the women who you had seen walking past you as you went into your prison camp – they were mainly Jewish women?

I think so. I've never seen such a sad-looking bunch. Terrible. They were certainly starved.

Before the planes arrived to collect the Allied POWs, Trevor had a discussion with an elderly German man.

Former prisoners of Belsen concentration camp cook their food over open fires, April 1945. These women, like those Trevor Mullinder describes seeing, were among the millions persecuted during the Nazi regime. IMPERIAL WAR MUSEUM, BU 3810

When we were waiting to be picked up by the Yanks to go back to England near this horrible mess, he was there with a little seven-year-old boy, and it's strange, I asked him straight out, 'Why did you people do this? You must have known that it was going on.' And he sort of hummed and ha'd a bit, and then he said, '*Alt mann, alt mann.*' Tapped the little fellow on the head, '*Kind, kind.*' He was an old man. '*Kind*', kid. '*Sprechen*', speak, 'Easy old man to die.' If he speaks, old man easily die. If he speaks *kind, mutter, vater* die. In other words, it's not just one man. The whole family would go. He was protecting his own, because if he spoke up the whole lot would end up in there.

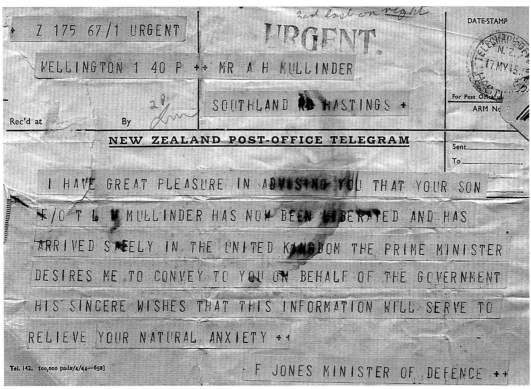

Good news at last. A telegram to Trevor's parents in Hastings telling them of his safe release in England after VE Day. TREVOR MULLINDER COLLECTION

A short time later, Trevor arrived back in England.

> Oh God, I was so pleased I just got down and kissed the earth, literally. Just down and kissed the earth, bloody glad to get back. And then of course we didn't realise that we stank so much, but we were put into tents and deloused, and we were taken from there by bus to Brighton and we were put into hotels. We were given some kind of clothing, to get rid of our old khaki and stuff like that. And we were given beds to sleep in, and most of us, we put our mattresses on the floor, because we couldn't sleep in those soft spring things, you see.

In England, Trevor learned that his pilot, Gerry Whincop, had also made it safely back, after being sheltered by a French family for about three months.

After the war, Trevor returned to New Zealand. He completed a BA in 1947 and stayed in the air force until 1966, when he went teaching. In 1946 he married

Trevor Mullinder, 2004.
ALISON PARR

Phyllis (known as Phyd) Davidson, and the couple have five children. It took Trevor a long time to settle down after his wartime experiences. For about fifteen years he would wake in a sweat from nightmares in which he was being hunted or strafed. Occasionally, more than 60 years after coming home, he still has them.

Gordon Forrester, 1939. GORDON FORRESTER COLLECTION

Gordon Forrester

ABLE SEAMAN GUNNER, HMS *OFFA*, RN

Whenever you got leave you lived that moment to the hilt, 'cos you never knew what's going to happen to you.

As a fifteen-year-old apprentice bootmaker in christchurch in 1938, Gordon Forrester had a hankering to go to sea. So he put his age up by six months and joined the New Zealand Division of the Royal Naval Volunteer Reserve, learning seamanship and spending time on the minesweeper *Wakakura* out of Lyttelton Harbour. When war was declared in September 1939, Gordon was mobilised immediately because of his time with the RNVR – at seventeen his ambition to be a full-time sailor was fulfilled when he joined the Royal New Zealand Navy. He served briefly on the *Achilles* and in August 1940 joined the *Monowai*, on which he served for nearly three years.

> The first brush I had with death was on the *Monowai*. We had a gun blow up and four blokes got killed, our shipmates. I was seventeen. It was a big shock. I even tried to go and look at them when they were dead, but I got as far as the door and couldn't go in 'cos they were put in a bathroom just along from my cabin, the bodies, when we were taking them back to Auckland.
>
> When I think back, it was sad at the time, but it was something that you accepted. They're gone. They got killed. The big worry was the guns they were on weren't safe. Most of the guns came from museums for the *Monowai*.

In the middle of 1943 Gordon travelled on the *Monowai* to England, where he was

Gordon Forrester in the Royal Naval Volunteer Reserve, on HMS *Wakakura* in Akaroa, 1938. GORDON FORRESTER COLLECTION

based in Plymouth and did further gunnery training. The following year he and a mate, Bill Thurston, joined the destroyer HMS *Offa*.

I'd had a very comfortable life up to then. The big difference on a destroyer was you had to sleep in a hammock. It was virtually the same as the *Achilles*, except more cramped. You're on top of each other. I'd been able to get over my shyness by the time I went over there, and it didn't worry me because you're with such close comrades. Especially with a destroyer, you're a lot closer to each other because of the danger and the cramped conditions you lived in. As soon as you go into a new mess deck, you're immediately made welcome. Bill and I got on very well with the English fellas. They welcomed us. Didn't treat us as foreigners.

But there were differences for the two New Zealanders to adjust to. The class system in the Royal Navy was marked, and Gordon was aware of strict divisions between men and their officers.

Pukkah, navy gentlemen. On a New Zealand ship it was there, because there is a line drawn between the officer and the rating. But I found that on the *Offa* they were 'up here' and you're 'down here'. No 'Gidday Forrester, how are you, how's things going?' No. The nearest I got to being friendly on the *Offa* was my divisional officer – I started a rugby team on there, and we used to go ashore in Scapa Flow and play with anybody who wanted to play us. And he, the divisional officer, was the half back and I was the captain.

So rugby gave you a level playing field?

Yes. Because on the field there's no rank. One particular game we were playing, he was forever getting offside. So in the finish I tailed him up and I got stuck into him. I said, 'I've had enough of you, you bastard, givin' free kicks away all the time' – this was the English officer, a lieutenant. I was the captain on the field. The upshot of it was, he called me into his office and asked me did I want promotion – would I go for leading seaman? I didn't want it.

As a seaman gunner, Gordon worked in a crew with six other people.

When action stations occurred you got up to your gun as quickly as possible. It was my job to make sure everything was working properly round the gun with the gun crew and keep them in hand. And when called upon to fire, make sure we got the right ammunition. There was two 4-inch guns forward, and one aft – and a 4-inch ack-ack. We wore our steel helmets and anti-flash gear and gloves. Anti-flash gear was like a balaclava, only it was white and just left your face showing. It just covered your head and your hands. If you got a flash it was supposed to stop you getting burnt.

A Royal Navy gunner in protective clothing at the sights of a 4-inch gun, 1940.
IMPERIAL WAR MUSEUM, A 1364

His first experience of sailing with the *Offa* was patrolling in the Atlantic and the Strait of Dover, on watch for German submarines and E-boats – small, fast vessels that fired torpedoes. On the first night out the *Offa* was attacked by a torpedo bomber.

> That was my baptism of fire. Frightening. I didn't know what the hell was going on. More so their guns firing than anything, 'cos my gun didn't fire. There was bang bang bang all around me and bloody Oerlikons firing away and attacked by that torpedo bomber and E-boats, I think it was. I thought, what the bloody hell did I volunteer for this for? But after a while you got to take it and it just became part of it.

The fear never goes away. But it's healthy, because it keeps you alive, fear. It makes you more careful. It makes you sure what you're doing. It's rather hard to describe when a ship's in action just how you will feel. There's always this churning in the stomach, it's always there. And I must confess that I did say a prayer just about every time. And I'm still here, so whether it helped or not, I don't know. You kept that within yourself. Because after every action is over, the bravado is there and you're more or less making jokes to get over it. Of course the adrenalin is flowing while you're in action, and then there's the come-down and that's when the cigarettes helped. Out come the smokes, and bring you back down to earth . . . out on the mess deck, and sometimes paying a call to the heads on the way – get rid of the churning. It's hard to describe being on a ship with all the guns firing and the noise, and of course if you're being attacked by the aircraft, the sound of the aircraft and their machine guns. That's what used to get me more than anything, the noise. You got used to it, but it was still there. Always that apprehension. That's why whenever you got leave you lived that moment to the hilt, 'cos you never knew when you were going to go out again, what's going to happen to you. There was always E-boats there, and we were having a go at them and they were having a go at us. We got one once, the forward gun got it.

What was that like?

Great, good, cheers, you could hear it all over the ship. One hit and boom, there was nothing left of it. Bastards. . . . they were the enemy. Two shakes, it could have been us. You had no compunction. You'd never ever seen the whites of their eyes when you're fighting at sea, even when you're dropping depth charges on submarines you don't give a thought to the people there, it's a submarine. And if we get the submarine, hurrah! That sub has probably taken care of hundreds of lives, a lot of ships in our convoy. You're sailing along, and boom, big smoke and flames, down it goes – being torpedoed. That's all you, and of course then we go into action to try and pick up the ping, an echo, and we do our run over it. And you can drop a lot of depth charges and not get that sub. Or you can get it and not know you've got it. It was just something you had to do. I'd never give any thought to, what, a hundred men down there. It was just a sub. We've got to get it. The same with the planes. There's a pilot up there. You never thought about the man, you thought about the plane – get that bugger. And E-boats – same thing, get it.

One night we were in action in the Channel, this is the night we got the E-boat, and we were coming up onto this E-boat, and the forward guns were firing but the gun behind us couldn't fire because there was a safety stop which stopped it firing over the top of our heads. I was bending down and the gun sheared the safety stop, and as I stood up, it fired right over my head. I thought we'd been bombed, and that was the shock of the shell. I couldn't see, I couldn't hear, my eyes were running, my nose was running and I thought it was blood. And they kept firing. Not only got one blast – two. When it was all over half my gun crew were deaf, and I got hauled up to the captain through not making sure that the gun crew had put cotton wool in their ears. Nowhere did anybody say we had to have cotton wool in our ears. So I got a reprimand. That was my first reprimand. You tried to get them to put cotton wool and they just tell you to go jump, 'cos I was only an AB [able seaman]. What saved me from losing my hearing was that I was wearing headgear. I was a rugby player and I played lock. In those days the locks had headgear with sponge-rubber ears that protected your ears when you were in the locking position in a scrum. That's what saved my ears. I always had that on. If I hadn't had that on it would have blasted my ears to nothing.

When the Royal Navy fleet prepared to leave southern England on the eve of D-Day, Gordon recalls that the event was not heralded in any special way.

Rumour is always there. I didn't think it was great that there was going to be an invasion, it was just something that we had to do and that was going to happen. We just carried out our duties as normal. Patrol the Atlantic, go out at night, come back the next day. Then all of a sudden we sailed and we were out at the mouth of Portsmouth Harbour and there were hundreds of ships, and I thought, hello, here it is – this is it. On board, the captain spoke to us over the intercom and said what was going to happen. That's when I did get keen and excited, when the actual invasion started. All of a sudden we took off. As far as the eye could see, ships, landing craft, warships, name it and they were there. I know it was dark when we got to the coast of France. We were starboard head of the armada, screening the head. We were leading them in. We watched the rocket ships go forward doing their thing, firing their rockets, all the hieroglyphics that went with the shelling. And then we turned and came back out again through the armada. And that's when I looked up and saw the *Monowai*. I was as excited as hell – 'There's my old ship. Oi, look at that, a New

Zealand ship!' Telling it all around, it was a New Zealand ship. She'd been converted into a troop carrier and she was full of troops, taking them in to land them.

In Portsmouth the *Achilles*, another of Gordon's former New Zealand ships, had spent months being refitted. Just before D-Day it had sailed out of harbour, heading down the coast for further repairs and passing the main fleet. The crew of the *Offa* had watched as the *Achilles* sailed away.

And of course they all give me the borax – 'Ah, look at that bloody New Zealand ship, it's turning tail, not coming with us.' All that carry-on. And that hurt. That's why I made a big thing when I saw the *Monowai*.

The *Offa* repositioned itself behind the main fleet off the French coast, and the crew were kept busy. They spent the next 24 hours screening for submarines and E-boats.

We were action stations just about a day and night. You spend a lot more time awake than asleep on a ship, especially when you're in action. Of course we weren't firing or doing anything, we never shelled ashore. My vivid memory of the coast is just a wall of fire, fireworks, like rockets and shells coming towards, ammunition coming towards and ammunition going away. The tracers and explosions, flashes of yellow and red. And the aeroplanes, towing the gliders and the gliders of course full of men. Magnificent. That night it was very dark, which emphasised the display. Once again I thought, gee that's great. I didn't think that underneath all that there were people getting killed. That's the way you exist in war. You'd never see anything like that again, not in a lifetime. Even a firework display couldn't do what I saw that night.

We were sailing along, and we came across this Dakota and it had its nose up and there was a bloke on the wing. We rescued him, we left the plane and took him aboard. I never got to talk to him to find out how many he had, how many were with him, was he the only survivor or what? I didn't even give that a thought. I can think about it now – Jesus, I hope the plane wasn't full of blokes. That was the first night.

There was a continual stream of traffic. The traffic was terrific for days. At one stage I was up there on lookout – it was a tugboat towing something. We were all saying, 'I wonder what that is?' Anyway, it was part of the Mulberry Harbour. That was the second or third day. The

Exhausted gun crew on board a Royal Navy ship snatch some sleep while they can.
IMPERIAL WAR MUSEUM, A 4207

second day, the battleships came, four of them. They came and they'd be maybe twenty miles off the shore and they all stopped in line, spread out. And we had to look after them, screen for submarine. All they did was fire their 15-inch, 16-inch guns ashore. I was quite impressed with this. Big ships firing those 16-inch shells. I was up on deck watching it, and I was that tired I lay down on the steel deck and went to sleep, 'cos I wasn't on watch or action stations then. I just went to sleep like a log. And I woke up and they were still firing!

At one stage the skipper decided to have a nosey, so we went in to the shore thinking that the occupation force had subdued the enemy. I'm on lookout on the starboard side, on the bridge, and next thing there's a big splash in the wake, and the skipper says, 'Full speed ahead!' It was a bloody shore battery firing at us. And here we are, 11-inch shells falling. I put me steel helmet on! I thought, God, blimey, they're firing at us. We got out of range and we signalled back to the shore, this is what happened, and next minute we see firing – our own shore guns wiped them out like a dirty rag. That's the only time I was a wee bit worried, 'cos you could see what happened.

How aware were you that you were involved in something historic?

I think I was just getting on with my job. Don't forget I was only twenty, although a hardened man by then. But I didn't have thoughts like that . . . that you're being part of the liberation army. I didn't realise that until after the war.

After the landings in Normandy, the crew of HMS *Offa* were allowed to go ashore for a taste of France.

They decided to give us a bit of leave to let us see France, because after all we'd helped recapture it. So they issued us with some francs, we went on leave, we walked ashore. We couldn't get far because it was all rubble, with the shelling and that, so they must have bombed it as well. You couldn't see much until we came across a little café / wine bar. We went into this wine bar to have a drink. 'What have you got?' He says, 'Calvados'. He was a Frenchman. We said, 'How much?' He said, 'How much have you got?' So we showed him our francs and he took the lot and we had a little glass of bloody wine. But we'd had a drink in France, which is what we wanted. We only had an hour or two's leave, it wasn't long. The biggest part of it was trying to dodge the American trucks that were trying to run us down. They don't like the English. You had to get out of their way, put it that way. You're walking along and they're heading towards you. You're not going to stand there. They think it's a great joke. 'Ah, ya limey bastard!' They called the English limeys. In London I'd say, 'Don't call me a bloody limey, I'm a New Zealander!

Gordon came home to New Zealand at the end of 1945 and retired from the navy the following year. He was among the servicemen from the Second World War who found the adjustment back to peacetime difficult.

Gordon Forrester, 2004. ALISON PARR

That meant I was going to be a civvy. I didn't want that. I wanted to
be a sailor. That was the whole aim of it. That's why I joined the navy.
The thought of becoming a civilian didn't make me very pleased at all.
Not wanting to go back to the boot trade, I had no skills. You've got to
understand that, having lived for the day, you don't hand that life away
easily, you carry it on in civvy street – and the comradeship was still in the
pubs. You'd spend all your day in the pub, with your shipmates, 'cos you
didn't want to let go. That's why I joined the army, probably. I just couldn't
accept coming back into civvy street.

In 1950 Gordon joined the Army Regular Force, serving for 22 years until his retirement as a warrant officer first class. In 1945 he had married Ethel Whittaker,

an Englishwoman who served as a WAAF in the RAF. The couple settled in New Zealand and had four children.

I'm pleased I was able to take part in D-Day. On the 60th anniversary I felt proud that I had been part of that. It probably took all that time to realise just what I'd done. At the time it was just doing my duty. The man up top said, 'We're taking the ship to France to help the invasion force, and you're going with me.' That was it.

Russell Clarke, 1944. RUSSELL CLARKE COLLECTION

Russell Clarke DFC

FLYING OFFICER, 485 (NZ) SQUADRON, FIGHTER COMMAND, RAF

It was a unit to be very proud of, and it's a magic number as far as I'm concerned.

LIKE MANY NEW ZEALAND PILOTS IN THE SECOND WORLD WAR, RUSSELL CLARKE first flew in a Tiger Moth. His early training, in 1942, was with the RNZAF on the Taieri Plains near Dunedin. He remembers that the trainees' huts were randomly dispersed over a 40-acre paddock – a precaution against a feared Japanese attack.

Russell was born in 1921 in Matamata and grew up on his family's farm. In his schooldays he watched a local farmer, 'Mad Mac' McGregor, a First World War pilot, perform aerobatics in a Gypsy Moth, never dreaming that one day he would fly himself. However, when war was declared he knew he did not want to join the army.

> I certainly didn't fancy the thought that I might be required to operate a rifle and a bayonet and be involved in hand-to-hand fighting. I thought that there was a bit of glamour involved with learning to fly, and being taught to fly at the government's expense, well, why not?

Following training at Taieri and Woodbourne, Russell left New Zealand to join the RAF in the United Kingdom, where he was eventually posted to Lincolnshire to train in Spitfires. In January 1944 he joined 485 (NZ) Spitfire Squadron. Technically, the new pilots were ready for operational flying.

> On that score, yes, we were prepared; we weren't prepared for the psychological side of the combat. It had all been newsworthy stuff right

from the start of the war, the part that the fighter aircraft were playing and the casualties that were occurring. Something of the nature of things I suppose we'd seen on newsreels on the screen, and so the big question in my mind, and I suppose in the mind of all the fellows like myself, was how we were going to measure up in that circumstance. So our first operational flights were . . . we were very keyed up to know what lay ahead of us. Each time we went up again, you know, the same thing was there. What are we going to meet up with, and how are we going to measure up to what transpires? I think we all recognised and made no secret of the fact that we were pretty nervous about what lay ahead of us.

Of course when you're airborne and you're over enemy territory you're sky-watching. Always something to do, so you were keyed up, but you were also busy enough that you didn't have too much time to sit and shiver in your boots or anything like that.

In early April 1944, 485 Squadron moved south in preparation for D-Day, becoming part of the Second Tactical Air Force (2 TAF). Russell gained experience in escorting bombers on daylight raids into France and Belgium, as well as dive-bombing and low-level bombing of strategic targets such as railway yards and V1 launching sites. The squadron was based at Selsey Bill, a promontory in the English Channel. Along with their ancillary ground staff, the men lived under canvas.

We were given a tent to erect and make ourselves at home as best we could, and we were told that if we walked through the woods we would find a little cottage. I think it was called Rose Cottage. It had been just a farm-worker's cottage and there weren't any great facilities there, I can tell you. That was the sergeants' mess, and alongside it the cook and his assistants were set up for providing us with meals. His cooking facilities were . . . basically it was a trench dug in the ground, might have been about 30 or 40 centimetres wide and possibly about 4 or 5 metres long, and there was a forced draught of flame driven along there and the thing was covered with steel plates. There must have been bottled gas or some form of inflammable spirit. So that's how they cooked our meals. We were given a folding camp stretcher and blankets, and one thing and another – and there was a bedroll that went with it.

The whole set-up was the squadron, the pilots and all the ground staff, and there might have been anything up to 200 of us. The ground crew were regarded with the greatest amount of admiration and respect, in that they kept the level of serviceability of the aircraft high. If we were called

Waiting for action. 485
Squadron at Selsey Bill
RAF base, May/June 1944.
RUSSELL CLARKE COLLECTION

to an early show, they'd been up already some time beforehand getting the
aircraft ready. They had to do what the circumstances called for, and they
did it marvellously well. They were very loyal to 485 Squadron.

From the moment the squadron was appointed to the 2TAF the men knew they
were destined for the invasion force in France. They also knew they would have to
continue operational flying from temporary bases – for the next year they would
be on the move.

We were taught to be mobile, and there was reason for that. We were
going to have to move up behind the army in Europe and move forward
as the army captured territory, to follow them. So that was one thing.
Secondly, they painted identification stripes on the aircraft, around the

fuselage back towards the tail, and on the wings, both above and below, there were broad white stripes. It was all intended to make us more visible to our own people, whether the gunners down below or other planes in the air.

Within a short time it became clear that D-Day was approaching.

From the air, returning from a sortie across the Channel, you would sometimes pass over portions of the south England countryside and see lines and lines of trucks on the side of the road, just sitting there. You couldn't fail to be aware of the build-up of material that was sitting there waiting to be transported across.

The task of the squadron during the invasion was to patrol Sword and Juno beaches, to support the landings there. But the men were given their orders only hours before the dawn of D-Day.

We were roused out of bed. It was somewhere before midnight on the night of the fifth, I suppose, and we were called to attend the intelligence section to be briefed, and at that point we were informed that it was going to happen the next day and what our role would be. The squadron would be split into two teams, each of twelve, and the first team would fly off at daybreak across the Channel and patrol for as long as their petrol would allow and return, at which point the second team would become airborne and take the job over, and we could expect that each team would do two trips, the squadron would do four sorties every day, twelve aircraft at a time. Our role was just to patrol up and down the beachhead, and we were just to be on the qui vive [the lookout] for enemy aircraft.

I was on the second team, so it might have been mid-morning before we took off. It was summertime and the daylight hours over there are quite extensive . . . the first team took off something like four o'clock in the morning, and we probably took off something like mid-morning. By this time the Channel was absolutely peppered with vessels of one sort or another which we, from time to time, took a glance at. We were still required to keep formation and also to keep lookout for enemy aircraft, so the sky-watching thing was always our first priority. But yes, I still remember the density of traffic on the Channel. Goodness knows where they'd all sprung from and what they were all doing, we had no means of knowing. It was probably quite well spaced out – there was no danger to

Time for a haircut. 485
Squadron, Merville,
France, September 1944.
RUSSELL CLARKE COLLECTION

the vessels in close proximity, but compared with the Channel that we'd
known the day before it was a very busy place. There was a lot of traffic.
And then some of the larger warships came into view the closer we got to
Normandy coast, and they were bombarding the coast, bombarding the
German emplacements behind.

We flew up and down along the length of the area that we were specified
to look after, and so we were just keeping position. And of course there
were lots of other squadrons doing the same thing, and how many Spitfires
there were above the beachhead area at any one moment, I don't really
know. But it wasn't only 485, that's for sure.

We didn't know just how much opposition we were going to meet
from the Luftwaffe. If they'd been fairly reticent up to this point, there
was a good chance they were going to be doing their best to hold their end
up when the time came, so we expected that there would be opposition.

'Bathing facilities' at 485 Squadron's camp in Merville, France, September 1944.

But once again it seemed to be always the other team that saw the action. And our team seemed to be getting all the quiet ones. In my log I wrote, 'Beachhead patrol, two hours 10. The big do. No joy. Called Operation Neptune.' That's the only entry for D-Day.

On the morning of D-Day, pilots from the earlier flight of 485 Squadron made history by being the first Allied airmen to shoot down enemy planes during the invasion. For the other flights in the squadron, this was frustrating.

Those that participated in that were hyped up, that's for sure. But the rest of us, we just had to possess ourselves in patience and hope that it happened to us next time. I suppose in a way we were relieved that we

Airman Mac McInness cooking corncobs in a petrol can, Merville, France, September 1944.
RUSSELL CLARKE COLLECTION

weren't being exposed to getting shot down, but at the same time we were feeling pretty frustrated that we weren't getting our chance to contribute.

And the next day, in my log, 'Beachhead patrol. Two hours. Chased two Focke-Wulf 190s to Le Havre.' That same day, D-Day+1, 'Beachhead patrol, two hours 05, nothing doing.' And so it goes on day after day, beachhead patrols, just a succession of them.

In the weeks after D-Day, the RAF began moving its aircrews to bases in Europe. In August, 485 Squadron travelled from Selsey Bill to Carpiquet in Normandy and set up their base under canvas. Within weeks the squadron's training in mobility was useful as another relocation followed, and in September a third, to Merville, near Armentières, where they spent the next two months.

The ground on which we pitched our tents, I don't remember it raining particularly much, but it just turned to mud such as you wouldn't believe, and it got to the point where we were up to halfway up our flying boots in mud until they managed to manufacture a few duckboards for getting ourselves to our tent lines. It was mud as I had never imagined. It wasn't as though we ploughed up the soil at all. It just turned to mud. And it made me realise just what it must have been like for the troops in the First World War. New Zealand troops were stationed in that area all round there. That's what they had to contend with . . . well, they have my sympathy more than ever.

We were young and we had good clothing. The mud was terribly unpleasant, no doubt about that – keeping ourselves clean, when I think back now I wonder what we did do to cope with it all. We usually managed to find somebody to do some laundry for us. There'd be a bathhouse in some of the French towns, and we'd make a pilgrimage to go and have a bath.

What about food – did you get any food from anyone?

Well, we scouted around on occasions and visited farmhouses and bought eggs, and I remember on one occasion buying a goose. We were pretty pampered, really. We were given extra rations as operational pilots, and we got chocolate given to us and packets of raisins and things, and we got parcels from home occasionally, not on a regular basis. Very often it would be a fruitcake. Very welcome, marvellous. And tins of condensed milk, sometimes packets of butter, but usually by the time it got to us it was a bit rancid, so it wasn't all that palatable. I don't remember what else we got in there but it was always welcome, especially the fruitcake. If they'd done nothing more than send us fruitcake, we would have been very happy.

When the squadron moved to Maldegem in Belgium at the beginning of November, they were spared a winter under canvas. Buildings were commandeered for the men to live in. They continued their task of supporting the Allied advance, bombing and strafing targets identified by the army. The squadron also attacked 'targets of opportunity', which were sometimes troop trains and trucks.

As far as we were concerned, we were rather detached from the human aspect of things. I mean we didn't see these trucks as being people that we were firing at. We were firing at inanimate objects and so it was . . . it was like a sport, really. We were just trying to take them by surprise and the Hun were very adept. If they had to move, they moved under cover of darkness and they had very little movement on the road exposed in daylight hours, so we had to hunt a fair bit to find anything that was worth attacking. But nevertheless I'm sure we were a real nuisance to them. The fact that we were there was stopping them from moving in the daylight anyway, which must have hampered their war effort to some extent.

Did you ever see any evidence of human life after you'd hit those targets?

There was one episode that remains in my memory. As I said, for the greater part we were rather detached from the person-to-person aspect of warfare, but on this occasion, and it was while we were in Belgium at Maldegem, there was an army at a fort up near the Scheldt Estuary. We knew it as Breskens, it was apparently a German fort. And we were quite repeatedly detailed to attack this jolly fort, and on one occasion another pilot who, on an earlier flight had picked up this group of German soldiers, not under cover in the fort, they were out in the field . . . he called up the rest of us to come along. And yes, I still remember that. These fellows were caught out in the open and all they had to protect them was a haystack, and they tried to shelter behind this haystack. And of course the aircraft would come round and attack from the other side, and they had these fellows going backwards and around and around the haystack. There must have been half a dozen aircraft circling around. So that was the nearest we came to the impact of this being a personal war. For the greater part we were rather detached from there, we were attacking trucks or attacking vehicles or attacking buildings or whatever.

How many Germans in the field would there have been, roughly?

There must have been about a hundred of them.

And so you could see them going down?

Yes, I suppose we could. You don't see it very clearly from the distance that we were at. You see them moving around, but whether you see them actually dropping from being hit, I can't claim to have done that. [Reading from his pilot's log] '19 October. Skip bombing . . . Found 100 Huns in a field and chased them around haystacks till Treble Two took over' – that's Treble Two squadron. 'Clean shoot.' In other words, used up all the ammunition.

I have vivid memories of what we were doing, and I think it brought home to me that there were people on the other end of what we were doing.

In the months he was based in Europe, moving from France to Belgium, then Holland and later Germany, Russell also became aware of the impact of the war on the continent – on its cities and people.

In Caen, that's in the Normandy area, when we were in Carpiquet, it was very, very evident there. The British had obviously bombed the daylights out of the whole place, and it was just rubble and destruction everywhere you looked. And as we progressed I suppose there was some damage, but it wasn't as concentrated as in the Normandy beachhead area – that was the target area.

In Holland, the squadron was based on an aerodrome at Gilze-Rijen which had been a German base for the previous three years.

In January 1945 we were very aware that the Germans, in retreating from these areas, had really just robbed the whole area of anything that was valuable to them in the way of foodstuffs or equipment or whatever, and I think any Dutch people that lived there at that time . . . that would stay with them as a memory of a very, very difficult time in their lives – that they were short of food, they were short of everything, and they were short of even firewood to stay warm, and it was a very cold winter. That stayed with me, made me aware of what was happening with the local population.
   I remember at one stage where this part of Holland had been liberated, whereas the north and north-west part of Holland had not been, and some of our group went on a day trip up to Amsterdam and took with them some of the chocolate bars that we were getting rationed, as bargaining materials for whatever they had in mind . . . I had no idea. But they came back with horrific stories of what transpired when people knew that they had these chocolate bars and they were getting absolutely rushed, almost bailed up against the shop windows with people wanting to acquire these. That's how desperate they were for food and it wasn't that it was a novelty, it was just that they were hungry.

During the last months of the war in Europe the squadron had little opposition from German fighter planes. However, on 1 January 1945 the Luftwaffe heralded the New Year with one final assault on their enemy. In Operation Bodenplatte they

In spite of the grimness of war-torn Holland, 485 Squadron airmen at Gilze-Rijen take time out to dance in the snow, January 1944. RUSSELL CLARKE COLLECTION

launched 800 fighter planes in a surprise attack on Allied airfields in Belgium and the Netherlands – and the Spitfires of 485 Squadron, then still based at Maldegem, were among their targets.

> We were very complacent, I must say, that we hadn't seen any sign of German opposition in the air for months. And it had been all our way, we were supporting the ground troops and doing what we pleased, without any thought of anyone interfering with us. We thought it was all our show. It was only a matter of pushing these ground troops out of France, Belgium, Holland and into Germany, and then we might get home. And surely the Hun must have known that he was a spent force . . . but for all that, he decided he was going to have one last crack, and he mounted this operation.
>
> The weather was not very wonderful, and whether it was because of the weather or because of other reasons, we were stood down. So we had spent the night and didn't have to get out of bed very early the next morning. It was probably about an hour after daybreak that we heard these planes circling.

Was there a siren of any kind, or an alert?

No, we just heard this gunfire, and it was coming from these German planes that were attacking our aircraft, and because we were so complacent, instead of dispersing our aircraft on the aerodrome here, there and everywhere, we had them all nicely lined up in rows. And so they had a field day, they just ploughed down the rows and put them on fire and dropped the odd bomb here and there and created a bit of noise and havoc, and we lost thirteen of our eighteen aircraft that morning.

Our quarters were about two miles away from the aerodrome, so there was no way we could get down there to do anything about it. The good news was that those same fellows who attacked us went on to the next target, and at that stage they happened upon an aerodrome where the RAF residents were in the air and they took a horrible beating, so the retribution was delivered by our friends along the road. We felt pleased about that.

What was it like when you got to the airfield and saw the destruction?

Oh, heartbreaking, really. Our beautiful aircraft just reduced to smouldering shells, unbelievable. We felt that we'd let ourselves down. Fancy letting that happen to our beautiful aircraft. But although we lost thirteen aircraft out of eighteen that morning, we were back fully operational within 48 hours, which is a tribute to the back-up supply arrangements that the RAF had. There were spares, there was probably a stockpile in Europe and other squadrons had spares that they could give us.

Operation Bodenplatte destroyed 224 Allied aircraft, but the cost to the Luftwaffe was steep – 237 pilot casualties and 300 planes.

For pilots on both sides of the war, danger was inevitable. In his 130 operational sorties, Russell was at risk each time he flew fighter sweeps, bomber escorts or armed reconnaissance. One of the squadron's most dangerous tasks was flying into heavily defended targets. In October 1945 Russell was awarded the DFC for these operations – attacks on places such as the ports of Antwerp in Belgium and

Opposite: The scene that greeted crews of 485 Squadron after the Luftwaffe attack on their base at Maldegem, Belgium, on New Year's Day 1945, when more than half their planes were destroyed. RUSSELL CLARKE COLLECTION

The Luftwaffe attack at Maldegem, Belgium, on New Year's Day 1945, as recorded by 485 Squadron's cartoonist. RUSSELL CLARKE COLLECTION

Flushing [Vlissingen] in Holland, where the danger to pilots was from ground fire.

> Flushing was a very, very heavily defended place. If you ever went anywhere near that, they threw the works at you. If we saw them, those little harmless-looking black puffs in the sky, I suppose you thought it was never going to happen to you anyway, but if they had started to come a bit too thick and fast, you just changed direction and changed altitude, then you were far less likely to get hit, and that's the simple response we always had, that we weren't confined to flying straight and level. If we saw it coming, we got out of the road or we took evasive action.
>
> Of course there were various levels of anti-aircraft fire. Down near ground level you were vulnerable to machine-gun fire, and a bit higher up it might be Bofors or cannon fire that might get you. And the other, the flak, the big stuff was up at some altitude, 15–20,000 feet or more. So there were various types of flak.

Russell Clarke outside his tent in Drope, Germany on VE Day, May 1945. The protruding object beside him is a makeshift chimney. Russell remained in Germany with his squadron on occupational duties until August 1945.

RUSSELL CLARKE COLLECTION

Russell was hit only once, while he was attacking a target on the Rhine in an operation he had been called into at the last minute. His was the twelfth aircraft in line, so by the time it arrived the German machine gunners had their sights well set. The task that day was to bomb as well as strafe, and the squadron's Spitfires had bombs attached.

> I didn't realise that enemy fire had hit me until I attacked the target, and I had a bomb under this aircraft alright, but in the lack of preparedness for the job I didn't throw the right switches to prepare the bomb for release. And so when I thought I'd bombed I hadn't. I still had this bomb underneath my aircraft, and when I got up after attacking the target with the strafing I realised that my oil pressure was dropping.
>
> They'd put a hole in my oil line somewhere, and that meant that I had a limited time before the engine would start overheating. Fortunately we weren't all that far from base, and so I gained what height I could and I made an approach. I started to pour white smoke, which is when

Russell Clarke, 2005. ALISON PARR

the engine overheated, so I cut the motor at that stage and went into
land, and I landed on the runway alright but unbeknown to me they'd
not only punctured my oil line but they had punctured one of my tyres.
This aerodrome, the Gilze-Rijen, had had a pretty torrid time from the
RAF while it was still in German hands, and although they'd patched up
one runway for us, the grounds surrounding the runway were just a no-
man's-land of bomb craters, so when I touched down and this flat tyre
took over I just veered off the runway in amongst all these bomb craters,
and then the thought occurred to me, crikey, I've got this big bomb
underneath there. All I could do was hold my breath, and we came to
rest and no harm done. That was one episode where the flak did catch up
with me.

On one occasion in his time with 485 Squadron, Russell Clarke led six aircraft on
operational duties. Later, when they were based in Germany on occupational
duties, he had the honour of leading the whole squadron in formation flying.

After the war Russell came home to work on the family farm. In 1949 he married Margaret Browne, a science teacher. Two years later they moved onto their own land, granted through a returned servicemen's ballot, a dairy farm near Te Awamutu which they ran for the next twenty years. The couple had four children. The Clarkes retired to Hamilton, where Russell is still active in the 485 Squadron Association.

It's part of me now, and of course the ongoing aspect of that is the association with the fellows with whom I served. It was a unit to be very proud of, and it's a magic number as far as I'm concerned. I value very much my having been associated with Squadron 485 and all that means in terms of people, the men.

But mind you, we were just boys. One thing that bothers me a wee bit is that, as the years go by, those of us who are still surviving are starting to be looked upon as some sort of heroes, and I keep on trying to reiterate that we were just the ordinary boys in the street in those days. And that given the time warp from that day to this, if you take any cross-section in the street, they'd have done the same thing as we've done. Just time and place determined that we were the ones that were doing it.

Ned Hitchcock, 1943. EDWARD HITCHCOCK COLLECTION

Edward (Ned) Hitchcock

FLIGHT LIEUTENANT, ELECTRICAL ENGINEER OFFICER, RAF

It was a terrible feeling that we were a little handful of men on the shore on a German-held area.

NED HITCHCOCK'S FATHER WAS AN ELECTRICAL ENGINEER WHO IN THE 1900S had laid telephone cables across the Atlantic. In the Second World War, Ned himself worked in a pioneering field of electrical engineering, manning radar units for the RAF. He was born in Christchurch in 1918 and graduated from Canterbury University College with an honours degree in electrical engineering. In 1940 the RNZAF was recruiting people to work in Britain with the RAF on coastal radar. Ned, one of 28 selected to go, had no idea what he was committing himself to.

> I don't think we knew much about it at all, because it was all cloaked with secrecy. We didn't know what it was that we were going for. After I'd had my interview, the British minister announced the existence of radio location [radar] and appealed to the Empire for trained men – then we deduced that was probably us. But of course that was all secret.

The detection of approaching enemy aircraft and ships was crucial to the defence of Britain, and central to this was the development of radar. The first radar station was opened in 1942 and from then on high-powered stations were built all around the coast. Ned found that the secrecy about radar he had experienced in New Zealand was also endemic in Britain.

> You'd have notices in pubs and cafés indicating, 'The enemy is listening'. It was extraordinary really. As far as radio location was concerned it had the

reputation of being the best-kept secret in the war. The classic story goes of the WAAF in England who was a bit fed up with where she was and applied for a posting, and they said, 'Well, where would you like to go?' 'Oh,' she said, 'I'd like to get onto the radio location centres, that sounds most interesting.' And they had to say to her, 'My dear, you're on one!'

Ned left New Zealand at the end of 1940 as a leading aircraftsman. He arrived in Liverpool with the other New Zealanders who were destined to work in radar, most of whom were amateur radio operators. His first posting was to the RAF Electrical and Wireless School at Yatesbury, Wiltshire. The secrecy continued.

> Yatesbury was a big camp, I think the number of people was about 4000. Across the field there was a barbed-wired enclosure round the secret radar training, and every morning we had to walk across the path to the secret place. Our exercise books were officially entered as secret documents and they were handed in at night when we finished. So you couldn't have a bit of swot at night, because your document was secret and held in there.

After completing his training course, Ned stayed on at Yatesbury as an instructor. But he was restless and frustrated that he was not involved more directly with radar. When applications were called for people with electrical engineering qualifications, despite his New Zealand degree, Ned came up against the British class system.

> I went along and said I wanted to apply for that. They said, 'Oh, you can't do that.' 'Why not?' 'Well, if you had a university degree you would automatically go in with a commission. You didn't go in with a commission therefore you can't have a university degree.' End of story. You're at the very bottom of the heap. You're not allowed to know anything. You're not allowed to do anything. You're not even allowed to speak out of turn. The commanding officer was an RAF regular and they seemed to dislike wartime volunteers, and he was an Englishman of the officer class and they disliked colonials – he was a real bastard who disliked most people, and so that was terrible. To live in England in the lower class is an incredible learning experience.

A bright aspect of this time for Ned was a friendship with a fellow instructor, Arthur C. Clarke, the scientist and author whose work includes *2001: A Space Odyssey*.

He was a tremendous personality. At that stage he was always known as Rocket Clarke because he'd been a member or even a founder of the Interplanetary Society. He was terribly keen on interplanetary travel, and when they first launched the V2 bomb he was excited because he'd calculated that this German rocket would be capable of escaping from the earth's atmosphere, and that was wonderful! Even at that stage he was doing a bit of writing, and he wrote a science fiction story about the idea of launching a satellite in space. So later he was saying, 'Why didn't I patent it?' He actually wrote, in science fiction, the concept of having a satellite stationary in space that would be able to be used for communications. Incidentally, he used to beat me mercilessly at table tennis.

Ned was eventually given a commission and became an electrical engineer, aircraft, with the rank of pilot officer. He wanted to join 75 (NZ) Squadron, but was posted instead to a Bomber Command base at Swanton Morley in Norfolk as officer in charge of the electrical section. From there he transferred to 60 Group – the section of the RAF responsible for the administration of all coastal radar stations in the United Kingdom. He travelled extensively around the Scottish coast and to some of the islands. In late May 1944 he was on a train with a couple of sailors who were talking about the likelihood of an Allied invasion of France.

I remember thinking, isn't it terrific, here they are sitting in a train talking to me, and just ahead of them they've got this fantastic operation in which they will be launched on the French coast against enemy forces. And I dismissed that from my mind, it wasn't in my territory at all. Got back to headquarters, got back to 60 Group and Norman Best, the squadron leader, put his head inside my office and said, 'Do you want to go over with the invasion, Ned?' And I said, 'Oh that sounds good.' That was it. And next morning he poked his head inside and said, 'You'd better come down, we've got to go and pick up our kit.' And then he explained to me that the high-ups had decided that for the radar units that were going to be landed on the forefront of the invasion, they would be under very considerable stress when they arrived, and they had decided that two experts should go in there for that critical start.

Two RAF radar units were assigned to the invasion – one to the British sector and one to the American. Ned and Norman Best were seconded to the Ground Control Intercept (GCI) radar unit that was going to Normandy on an American landing craft heading for Omaha Beach.

An RAF coastal radar tower in the United Kingdom, under the administration of 60 Group, to which Ned Hitchcock was assigned. IMPERIAL WAR MUSEUM, CH 15174

We reported to Camp D2 near Bournemouth, an American-run camp, and it was an experience. All over the camp there would be American soldiers practising baseball, throwing a ball backwards and forwards. The discipline was very strict. To try and conceal the camp from the air you could only walk on designated footpaths – apparently a shortcut is so wonderfully visible from the air and gives away all sorts of secrets. And the meals were superb – awful lot of fried food, roast pork and things like that. I think the RAF food was scientifically designed. It was simple. This was American food. It was very pleasant for a change after the RAF limitations. The catering officer at one stage was ex-Lyons food chain and really knew his stuff, and he sometimes had salmon flown down from Scotland.

Everybody was that busy. They were totally puzzled as to what the hell we were doing there. It was a very great embarrassment being part of a secret operation. They couldn't imagine what we were doing, and of course we couldn't say. You were being swept along. You didn't really have anyone to talk to or ask about it, and we were totally abnormal – two officers from 60 Group, seconded to join a unit like that.

Ned and Norman Best were given no training in the American unit, but they were equipped with gear that included an escape map, French and German phrase books, and a revolver. It was only when he received his kit that Ned became aware that what lay ahead might be very dangerous, but he was able to suppress his anxiety.

My defence was that I avoided letting my imagination run away with me. You were issued with blue battledress which had been impregnated with chemicals to make it resist gas. This issue, full of anti-gas, was terribly hard to wear, and it was a reminder that we didn't know what Hitler was going to do in the last moments of desperation with the successful invasion. And gas was only one danger, of course. The one that lay at the back of my mind was that they were going to pump oil onto the sea and set fire to it. So sitting at the background there was always a slight concern about what was going to happen. And you got little reminders like the gas-impregnated clothing all the time. We were issued with assault-type respirators, which were American. They were contained in a rubber bag which folded over to be waterproof and they strapped on your chest, and we didn't know, of course, that they were going to be excellent lifesavers if we happened to be in the sea.

We were to be totally independent for 24 hours, carried your own food and everything else. You weren't dependent on any support for 24 hours you were on your own, and included in the issue were two condoms! This was our introduction to the American war.

Omaha Beach, the sector of the Normandy coast to which Ned's unit was assigned, was more than 10 kilometres long. Like all the other beaches on D-Day it was divided into code-named sectors. Ned's unit was scheduled for a section called Dog Red. His only instruction was that he would make the landing in a truck driven by a Canadian radio mechanic. In the final days before D-Day, Ned checked out the truck and was disconcerted to find that it had no high-level exhaust, leaving it vulnerable to stalling in deep water. However, as they set off across the Channel he again staved off anxiety by exercising what he calls 'thought control'.

I didn't allow my thoughts to run. I'm not a person who gets excited over things. On the other hand it was incredibly interesting, everything was happening, and of course the invasion ahead of us was a great unknown – I think thought control is the key to it.

We were just bunged on the landing craft and you found your own cosy corner to go to sleep, and I think the thought control had a wonderful beneficial effect in that I slept on that deck under a blanket and woke up in the morning, so I was quite impressed with myself. I woke up and there was the French coast at dawn and we peered at the coast – there was a bit of smoke rising, something had been happening there. We were just one of the five vessels. Norman Best was on the jeep with all the top-level people and the wing commanders, and they were supposed to be the recce party that went ashore first. For some reason or other our boat went in first, and

American troops under enemy fire shelter behind obstacles in the shallows on Omaha Beach on D-Day. Behind them, landing craft attempt to make it to shore. This is one of eleven surviving photographs taken during the landing by the eminent photographer Robert Capa. IMPERIAL WAR MUSEUM, AP 25724

as we approached the shore I saw this realism of war. There was an explosion and a man's figure went up in the air. You know, you read the term 'blown up' – this is right in front of our eyes. And then we were getting a bit nearer the shore and I think that I was perhaps getting a bit apprehensive. We had an American observer on board who had been in the landings in the Mediterranean and was assigned to us to be a general observer. And I gather he said, 'God, that beach hasn't been taken – the last thing they want ashore there is a gang of people with radio aerials', and he turned us around and we went out to sea again. I'm quite sure that I felt greatly relieved. We stood out to sea all day with the navy firing over our heads and bombarding the shore. You couldn't really see anything on shore except, I think it was a clock tower on a building. All of a sudden that disappeared. And those who knew said, 'Oh, that was being used as an artillery observer spot so the navy has disposed of it.' Otherwise there was nothing exceptional in it. I suppose there are always a few fires burning. There was nothing significant, any more than in the old days you used to see fires on the Canterbury Plains. And so we stood offshore – this was still D-Day, and the navy fired over our heads and we could see the bursts ashore.

And then I had another night sleeping on the deck, and at some stage next morning we set off towards the shore. There was a boat that I could describe as a pilot boat and it was tossing vigorously in the sea, and my impression is that the loudhailer said, 'What wave are you?' Then the voice said, 'Alright – in you go.' So we set off ashore. When we were near enough to the shore the order was given to get into the radar trucks and start the engines, and that's when I first met the Canadian. So we sat in the cab and he watched the vehicle in front of him going up and going down and getting away, and then it was our turn.

How far out from the beach?

Pretty hard to say, it was quite a distance.

So you knew you were going to have to drive through water?

Oh it was a wet landing, yes. And we plunged down the ramp into the water and there was no problem, the waterproofing was working, and we chugged away and drove perfectly normally towards the shore, and then I think I got a bit disconcerted that the water, instead of getting shallower, was getting deeper. It came up inside the cab and we were up to about our middle and I anticipated that the engine would give up at any time, and it stopped. I was convinced it would never go again.

As I remember, we sat there sort of paralysed. How could it possibly be that I, Ned Hitchcock, could be sitting in a stalled truck, in deep water, in a rising tide with nothing but an enemy-held beach ahead? How the hell did this happen to me? Just at that moment a wonderful Thorneycroft truck, which was a really big military vehicle and high above the water, steamed past us with a bow wave. He just steamed past and the driver reached up with a great big grin under his tin hat and he gave us the fingers! And this sort of broke the ice and we roared with laughter, that gorgeous grinning face. I'm sure he must have been a Cockney, that derision – the awful situation we were in. Anyway I said to the Canadian, I'd wade ashore to where we had a rescue vehicle – 'I'll get a cable and bring it up and they will tow us in.' So I waded ashore, got the cable. It was only up to our waist, there wasn't any difficulty, and very soon I appeared to be in shallow water and I dragged the cable back and hooked it onto the front, and eventually we began to move. And then there was some agitation from ashore, I think people were indicating that they couldn't pull it.

I sat in the cab on my own wondering what the hell to do next. The Canadian had taken off. The tide was rising and I don't think there was anything that I could do except sit there and feel the water rising, and when it got to the stage that the water was out of my depth I realised that if I wanted to get ashore there wasn't really anything else to be done, I would have to swim. And that's when I set off to swim ashore. That assault respirator strapped on my front was probably a great help. I think it must have been the flotation of the respirator, it was in a sealed container.

Were there any signs of wounded people around at that time?

Not until I was wading deep – there was one of our team there, one of the officers in the water, lapping gently. He was obviously an RAF uniform and he was obviously one of us. He would have been probably drowned if he was injured.

He was dead in the water?

He appeared to be, yes. Shelling was going on and my impression was they were picking off the vehicles. If vehicles had got ashore they shelled them,

American troops help a wounded soldier on Omaha Beach on D-Day. IMPERIAL WAR MUSEUM, EA 26319

and obviously the two Thorneycrofts were picked off and because they carried oil for the diesel, when they burnt, they burnt. They were burning fiercely as I came towards the shore, and a van was obviously exposed to fire. There was an American soldier taking refuge underneath that van – I think he was wounded. It looked as though the van would burst into flame at any moment so I said I'd pull him out, and that was a vivid memory, talking to this bloke. He took my hand, and it was quite a feeling in that desperate situation. He was in pain and the water was rising, and he took my hand and I pulled him out. There was nowhere to put him, really – but I got him away from the burning van. I climbed into the van, started the engine and drew it forward. There was nowhere for it to go because the beach was shut off with barbed wire. That's where I had listened to the shrapnel tearing through the air. There were some canvas sides on some of our vehicles, and I heard a tearing sound.

The impression we had was very much of emptiness. We weren't going ashore, as I had imagined, in company with a vast number of Americans. We were all on our own. There was nothing to do but see if one could get off the beach. I had no entrenching gear, because it was all in my kit in the truck. It was a terrible thing having the feeling that we were a little handful of men on the shore in a German-held area. The only thing I remember, which is a ghastly thought, there didn't seem to be anybody else around – and then the tanks came along the beach from the left, and I remember the ghastly sight of the tanks rolling over the dead. There were dead soldiers on the beach, bodies on the beach, and I suppose the tanks couldn't dodge them. I don't know if the tank drivers could even see them. These were American tanks. They must have been ones that landed on the main beach and came along the beach. We were thrilled to bits that there was somebody else.

There were two burnt-out wrecks of the Thorneycroft, and there's every chance that my smiling friend, the Cockney, was in one when it took the shellfire . . . the sheer chances of it happening after that glorious greeting. He went on and had every chance of being extinguished a few moments later. So that's a sobering thought, because if we had gone ashore we would have undoubtedly been picked off by German artillery. The extraordinary chances that took place. Our stalling probably saved our lives, instead of being the disaster that I thought it was.

I went up to the beach line under shelter of the trees because there was sporadic sniper fire coming from the hillside. There was very little we could do there except to dodge, and you soon learned you walked vigorously – I think when they are using telescopic sights they can pick you up if you're still, but if you walk vigorously they can't do it – so we learnt to walk vigorously from one shelter to another. One of our men got a bullet through the nose. It went through one side and came out the other.

During the landing twelve men from Ned's party were killed and 40 wounded.

We were able to rig a van up as an ambulance, and we collected the wounded and put them into this van to get them off. I think they were mostly shrapnel wounds. This of course was terrible, they were all thirsty and wanted water and all I had was my relatively small water bottle. I was able to give them water from that and I'm sure I must have got some more water from somewhere. Some of the Americans that were lying around were unconscious.

Ned had been told there would be a beach master and medical orderlies when they landed, but there was no help of any kind. Later rumours suggested that the American beach party may have been held back because landing was considered too dangerous, but he feels they were probably busy on other more heavily defended sectors of the beach. He eventually found his squadron leader, Norman Best, who had got ashore in a jeep with all his gear, which included two blankets.

> I had come ashore with what I was standing up in – my kitbag was out there in the vehicle, so I borrowed a blanket from him and we slept under a hedge in front of what was obviously a beach cottage in its peacetime days. And rumour had it that there were six German soldiers taking refuge inside of it who weren't at all ferocious. I think they were scared stiff. I don't have any recollection of discomfort. I slept in wet clothes with one blanket on the ground.

The section of Omaha Beach where Ned landed on D-Day+1. In the centre are the remains of the two burnt-out Thorneycroft trucks that were shelled as they drove onto the beach. Low tide exposes the underwater obstacles. US NAVY, NATIONAL ARCHIVES 80-G-45714

Did you have anything to eat?

Well there was this magnificent component of the K ration. It was concentrated food, it was mainly dried fruit with presumably a few other things in it and it was absolutely magnificent – it was so high-power and it was absolutely perfect for that situation, because all we needed was food to keep going. We didn't really care what it was.

Next morning Ned and the RAF group moved a little further up the beach and found an American vehicle with a radio. Until then, they had no idea what had happened in the landings, and in fact wondered if the invasion had been a failure. They feared they might become prisoners of war.

We were pretty worried about being grilled on the secret radar. We were a little handful of RAF in the middle of the American sector, all by ourselves. Then we got into this little grassy spot with this American vehicle and a loudspeaker going and quite a crowd around it, just listening to the BBC, telling us the invasion was a wonderful success. We were there on the spot.

The Americans supplied Ned with fresh clothing.

We were in the blue and the American commander said, 'I cannot guarantee that my men won't mistake you for Germans, because your blue is too similar to a German field grey, particularly if you got a bit of dust on it.' The good guys were in khaki and the bad guys were in blue! Shortly after the landing they had sufficient equipment to invite us to equip ourselves with khaki, and we suddenly transformed ourselves. We went up there and they laid out a whole lot of stuff. I got a beautiful white jacket which was just perfectly comfortable and must have been very smart. I don't know whether it was for wearing for dinner ashore – I just couldn't believe that these blokes had just come ashore and they could let us have access to all these clothes. I had a pair of ginger trousers and a shirt.

The vehicles from the RAF unit that reached the shore safely stayed in the same area for several days.

I think it must have been the next day the first of our replacement vehicles was coming, and I was sent to down to guide some of these in and I went down in American ginger pants and my nice white jacket.

There was a sort-up of the stock we'd got and what we lost, and the headquarters were in touch by radio and assessed what we hadn't got and those replacements were sent. I think the radar went on the air about D-Day+4. We had to cobble it all together and get it going. We had one of our generating plants with shrapnel through the radiator and we had another one with shrapnel through the petrol tank. And so that was very good – the petrol tank and the radiator were swapped over and we had one operating vehicle.

The men in the unit decided that they should make contact with the owner of the land they were on, and Ned was assigned this task.

I was the only one who was willing to admit any knowledge of the French language, so I was sent off to deal with this. I have a clear memory of friendliness and affability, which is not altogether to be expected from French country people, particularly as we had involved them in more war and damage. We had a discussion over the language – here was I with my schoolboy French trying to tell him that we were going to disperse heavy trucks all over his farm, and we had a discussion about what we called these – and I learnt a new French word, 'camion' – heavy vehicle. So that was the atmosphere that I remember from this, the friendliness of a stranger talking to this peculiar bloke who's just come out of the sea.

For a few days Ned and Norman Best moved between radar units that were being established, then headed back to England, hitching a ride on an American LST. In September Ned was again assigned to a radar unit heading for Normandy, this time to Sword Beach. He was much more confident than during his first landing in France.

Oh well, we were old hands, we knew the ropes. The ship came in and beached and we had a bulldozer that piled up sand in front of the ramps. It was difficult to get it down onto the beach so the sand was piled up so the vehicles could drive off. It was a bit of a contrast to leaping off the vehicle way out at sea.

As the Allies advanced across Europe, Ned was sent on other assignments to work on radar. He spent some months in Belgium and still remembers the remnants of war.

Ned Hitchcock, 2004.
ALISON PARR

There were burnt-out vehicles, and at one stage there were lots of dead horses – I do remember that, the dead horses. The Germans were very much dependent upon horse-drawn [transport], they weren't entirely mechanised. As we got to the industrial area in Belgium there were coal heaps and slag heaps. After beautiful northern France and the green countryside, my heart was sinking, this is where we're going. Of course, we were not to know that the people would be so warm.

After the war Ned Hitchcock returned home and worked as an engineer with New Zealand Railways for twenty years, and later as technical director for the Standards Association. In 1950 he married Joan Bull, an English nurse, and the couple have two sons. The family lived for two years in Malaya where Ned worked for the

Colombo Plan. A consulting engineer until his retirement, in 1980 he completed a PhD in technological law.

Ned still marvels at having had the chance to contribute to D-Day so directly.

> I think it was wonderful to be involved. That was an extraordinary bit of luck – the whole astonishing sequence of going down and joining the American camp, the landing, the swimming ashore, the whole thing. So totally and utterly improbable, and yes, it was exciting. I wouldn't have missed it for anything. It's easy enough to say that when you come out the other side.

Jim Pollok, 1944. JIM POLLOK COLLECTION

Jim Pollok

LIEUTENANT, HMS *RAMILLIES*, RN

The captain comes on the blower and tells us that we're heading
for Normandy . . . . and it's then he used the famous words – 'And
I shall be wearing the Maori skirt'.

JIM POLLOK WAS BORN IN INVERCARGILL IN 1918. WHEN THE SECOND WORLD WAR
began he was studying science at Otago University before transferring to Lincoln College to begin an agricultural science degree. At that stage he had no idea
that the hours he spent in physics lectures would help to equip him for his role in
the war. A year later Jim saw an advertisement in *The Press* calling for volunteers
for the Royal Navy, 'for a confidential job under arduous conditions'. He put his
name forward.

> I was completely in the dark. When we were called up we were called up
> in civvies and, at the end of 1940, we went to Auckland University in the
> summer vacation. Something was in the offing and when we got there, lo
> and behold if it isn't electronics. All this electricity and magnetism that I'd
> learned at Otago all of a sudden became very important. But anyway, we
> had an odd sort of a chap leading us through the elements of electronics,
> and then just in the last week after the two or three months they spilt the
> beans – here is a wonderful new electronic device that can see through the
> dark, through the murk, through the smokescreen, and can give the range
> and bearing of either ships or aircraft.

Was it called radar at that stage?

No, it was called Radio Direction Finding (RDF). And then they said,
well with all this high-flown stuff we'd better make you into sailors. So

they shipped us over to HMS *Philomel*, which was then a hulk tied up at Devonport, a cruiser from the First World War, but no longer seaworthy, and there we scrubbed decks with the seagulls screeching overhead and we learned to tie knots, and most importantly of all how to dress ourselves up in bell-bottoms to make us into real sailors. I was not yet a pukkah sailor, I was as raw as they come. I was really a landlubber. All the people in the course, we chummed together fairly well.

The eighteen young men in Jim's group had been recruited to work as radar technicians on coastwatching stations around New Zealand. But Jim's future lay offshore. At the beginning of 1941 the Royal Naval Volunteer Reserve (RNVR) – also known as the Wavy Navy because of the wavy sleeve bars worn by its officers – needed men for radar work on the HMS *Achilles*. Jim was surprised and delighted when he was accepted.

This officer looks us over and he says, 'I need four of you to join the *Achilles*, immediately. You, you, you and you.' And I happened to be in the firing line by great fortune, along with my three companions. And so we went. Picked up our kitbags and hammocks and saw the doctor and up the gangplank, and we were no sooner on board than the jolly ship backs off and out to sea again. So in one sudden swoop I'm whipped off to sea. I was very excited about going to sea. I took to being at sea, I loved it. It's the whole ocean environment, the motion of the ship. There're wide open spaces, there's a horizon. There's the spaciousness, there're clouds in the sky, you're close to nature. The *Achilles* was a relatively small cruiser. So it felt the motion of the sea, and I just loved everything. I just loved the kind of freedom of the ocean.

We used to argue that the Royal Navy, the pukkah navy, knew how to sail a ship. They knew the engine room, they knew the bridge and they knew the gunnery and they knew everything about navigation, and they could sail the ship. But when it came to one or two little exceptional things outside the square, that was when the Wavy Navy came into its prominence because its sailors were all volunteers, they were drawn from all walks of life. You could have an artist, you could have a schoolteacher or whoever, a poet. They could all come and have a go, and that's where you got the little bit of thinking outside the square.

For the next six months the *Achilles* was home for Jim and his fellow recruits. Their job was to sit in a small, dark room and watch green blips on a radar screen,

One of the first radar sets developed for the RNZN, installed in HMS *Achilles* in May 1940. The rapid development of Radio Direction Finding, or radar, was vital to the Allied war effort. Work on radar began secretly in New Zealand before the war, led by Dr Ernest Marsden, a physicist and then Director of Scientific Development. Radar sets for use on ships were designed at Canterbury University College, with additional work being done at the Radio Development Laboratory at Wellington East Post Office. A research engineer, Lieutenant S.D. Harper, was employed to work with a small team of scientists who further developed sets to increase range and accuracy. At the end of 1940 the navy recruited eighteen young men to train as RDF operators. It was this scheme that introduced Jim Pollok to life in the navy. ROYAL NEW ZEALAND NAVY MUSEUM, AAF 0062

reporting what they saw to the ship's bridge. The four RDF operators took turns at watches – four hours on, eight hours off. Jim had no problem concentrating on the job.

> We were on our mettle because this was the very first hand-built radar set and it was all valve electronics, so it could fall over at any time just like a light bulb. By the time I joined the ship it was just operating in New Zealand, Australian, Pacific waters. So we didn't have a lot of enemy

around. It was all fairly straightforward. But lack of sleep was one of the prime problems. Any real sailor is nearly always short of sleep in wartime. I was a bit short of sleep, but everybody was. You talk about getting your head down, well it's absolutely for real. I mean if you want naval language, getting your head down was any opportunity you had to get a wee bit of sleep – a godsend.

Those six months on the Achilles, *how would you describe them?*

It was formative because it introduced me to the sea. You bet it did. You sling your hammock, you're fast asleep, and then you have to be woken up and get to action stations. And a petty officer or a chief petty officer comes along and he shakes you, 'Wakey, wakey, rise and shine, the day is fine!' Gives you a good old rattle. If you don't wake up they give you a bit of a punch, or if they really have to they tip you out. I was a pretty mild sort of a

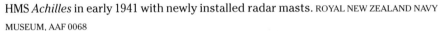

HMS *Achilles* in early 1941 with newly installed radar masts. ROYAL NEW ZEALAND NAVY MUSEUM, AAF 0068

sailor. I was a young fellow with a wee bit of knowledge of electronics, just enough to be able to operate a radar set.

This radar thing had a kind of glamour about it because it was hush-hush. I can recall quite distinctly once coming into Wellington Harbour, and none other than Sir Ernest Marsden would come down to the ship to check out the radar set with Lieutenant Harper. We were important people!

After six months, Jim was told he was being sent to England to serve in the Royal Navy.

I was over the blinkin' moon. I thought it was the most wonderful thing in the world. Well, the UK's the other side of the world, that's where the war is, this is prior to the Japanese entering into the war. Also, back when we were a British dominion, we were all very loyal and that's the home of the Royal Navy. England is England. That's where my forebears come from, England and Scotland. That's the most natural thing in the world, for me to want to go there. Just a pure gift. I'm told that I'm no longer an RDF operator, I am an RDF mechanic. I'm supposed to be able now to fix these things. I was made a killick [a leading hand]. It was a real promotion. I got an anchor on my arm. My pay increased, everything goes up, but the responsibility now becomes a little frightening and the blinking rig is horrible. And they shipped me over to England like that.

Jim arrived in England towards the end of 1941 and was sent on a radar training course. From there he was posted for six months as an instructor at the technical radar school at HMS *Valkyrie*, a shore base on the Isle of Man.

I wasn't the only New Zealander of this group that went over – there were seven or eight of us. They were all the same as me, they'd all been pro-moted overnight into mechanics and now into radar mechanic instructors. You were plunged into jobs we hadn't done before, that's for sure.

The New Zealanders continued their rapid advancement when they were pro-moted to temporary probationary sub-lieutenants and sent to Portsmouth for more training in radar.

And now a Royal Marine servant with a silver tray brings us our gin and lime. It's a new life, a different kind of life altogether. I don't sling my

hammock any longer. And I got a proper, pukkah naval uniform. I went to
Bond Street, Gieves Naval Tailors, you go along there and they measure
you up, proper tailors, and they fit you out with a handcrafted naval
uniform. But this little thin stripe doesn't carry much weight you know.
Not in the hierarchy. You're still, as it were, on the bottom rung, but it's a
different ladder.

The captain of the Signals School appointed them to different posts. Jim was sent
to the battleship HMS *Ramillies* as radar officer.

Just me, Wavy Navy, temporary acting sub-lieutenant appointed as Radar
Officer HMS *Ramillies*, refitting in Devonport. I travelled down there and
then reality hits you, clean before the eyes – just before that Plymouth had
been bombed, so it was simply a city of rubble, and I can remember picking
my way over the great chunks of masonry to get to the dockyard where the
ship was. It struck me as for real. The war in Europe was real, the war in
England was real. When I say the war, I mean the bombardment.

Had you had a real sense of that before you got to Plymouth?

Oh no, not at all. It was pretty dastardly, pretty dramatic, pretty impressive.
I remember somewhere along the line calling in at a NAAFI [Navy, Army
and Air Force Institutes] shelter, which was really just tarpaulins rigged up
and very dark and dim inside, and all blacked out outside, for a cup of tea.
And there was the old English cup of tea as strong as it comes, and you
down that and then you continue on your way. I picked my way down to
the dockyard. Nothing had been cleared up. The bombing was recent.

At the time Jim joined the *Ramillies* it was undergoing a refit that lasted for three
months. As well as older equipment, a new radar set was installed, long-range surface-warning radar that was state of the art.

It put the Royal Navy streets ahead of its opponents. So here I am, still a
rookie, and I have this absolutely top-class surface-warning set. I was very
excited about this. In practical terms it meant you had a much less anxious
time of it. You could depend on this set. It was on the top of the mainmast
– in order to get maximum energy to the aerial they actually built the
transmitter on a platform on the mainmast about 100 feet up in the air,
so I made a point of always climbing up the mainmast to see the chaps

operating the set in the middle of the night to make sure that they were happy and the set was going alright.

I had a sub-lieutenant to help me and there were three petty officer radar mechanics. So we made a team of five that had to keep the sets going. Then we had about 50 operators.

Soon after the ship went to sea, Jim was promoted to lieutenant. He quickly developed positive feelings for the *Ramillies*.

It was a happy ship. It's indefinable. The people in it make it a happy ship, and a lot depends on everybody. If you come onto the upper deck, from the captain down, everybody contributes to making it a happy ship, the morale in the ship, the general atmosphere. We had a good long time to shake down because we were at least three months in dock and so you get to know one another.

Crew on the battleship HMS *Ramillies*, 1941. IMPERIAL WAR MUSEUM, A 6099

A ship is a marvellous thing. A ship won't work unless you're all working – if you're all contributing, it's absolutely marvellous. The moment you leave port you are on your own, you either sink or swim. I mean the whole show has to work, it's an independent unit that's buzzing with activity. Once you put to sea you're on your mettle, because you are now responsible for staying afloat on the ocean. In actual fact you are a floating magazine. You have all this enormous high-explosive cordite and shells stored in your magazine, and you only have to be hit and the whole thing goes up. But you know you're oblivious, you don't even think about it, you don't think that you can be sunk, it's the last thing you think of.

For several months the *Ramillies* was based with the Eastern Fleet at Mombasa on the coast of Kenya. Then, unexpectedly, they were on the move.

We think we're in the Indian Ocean for the rest of the war. All of a sudden a signal arrives from the Admiralty to say the ship's got to come back to England, and after that it's all a question of what's up? Rumours are rife, especially on the lower deck. We were obviously going back for a purpose – they wouldn't pull us out of the Eastern Fleet – we'd only just arrived four or five months before. And there was all the talk about a second front. The word got around that maybe we were in for something worthwhile. I was made aware then that things were afoot, because as a radar officer I had to know a thing or two, and so I knew that we were heading for Normandy, eventually. You can't disguise the fact. Eventually we're up at Scapa Flow and all of a sudden we find that we're visited by First Lord of the Admiralty and lined up on the quarterdeck to meet him. What's he doing coming out to see us? We'd never seen him before in our lives. And then before we could say Jack Robinson, King George the Sixth arrived, well you know a King doesn't normally come, so by now you couldn't sort of hide things. And blow me down if we don't get a signal to say that Lord Montgomery will be on board the *Howe* and that he wants to address all those who are free to attend, and I get in a cutter and go across to the *Howe*, which is the number one modern battleship, and there standing on a capstan is Lord Montgomery, and he hops up there and tells us we are in for glorious things and that the German fighters are great fighters but the British fighters are better ones.

By now we are getting pretty close, but at the same time we're exercising every day, just about. We sail out to sea and we let off these enormous guns, 15-inch, which we hadn't actually fired before. They're big guns. They

King George VI inspects sailors on HMS *Ramillies* just weeks before D-Day, 1944.

let off a big bang. I have a friend who was in landing craft at Normandy and he referred to the fact that he could hear these things going off overhead. We were practising on targets out at sea. And then we went down to the Clyde and we did the same thing. This is going to be a bombardment, and so what you do is you have a fixed target and now you have to locate that target as accurately as possible and fire at it with these enormous guns.

On D-Day the *Ramillies'* position in the bombarding force was off Sword Beach, along with another battleship HMS *Warspite*, and HMS *Roberts*. The ships were on the most vulnerable and therefore the most strongly defended flank of the force. Their primary task was to knock out enemy coastal defences.

We were all keyed up. We'd been working up for a couple of months at least. Off the Isle of Wight there was a great collecting centre of naval vessels, not just warships – which are there in their hundreds, because you've got battleships, cruisers, destroyers and frigates all armed to the teeth – but you've also got landing craft full of infantrymen, landing ships which carried landing craft hoisted out, you've got landing craft tanks, carrying tanks, you've got a whole armada of vessels. So we all assembled.

Visitors gather on HMS *Ramillies* at Pipitea Wharf, Wellington, January 1940, before it escorts New Zealand troops to the Middle East. It was during this visit that Ngati Poneke presented the captain of the *Ramillies* with a piupiu (flax skirt). WAR HISTORY COLLECTION, ALEXANDER TURNBULL LIBRARY, DA-07123

It was in the evening that the captain, Captain Middleton, comes on the blower and tells us that we're heading for Normandy. We now know from the horse's mouth that we really are crossing the Channel and tomorrow morning at dawn we will be opposite the beaches of Normandy. And in the morning we will be at action stations. I had a false sense of security as far as the ship was concerned. It's so big. You just feel so secure in such a large vessel which doesn't feel the motion of the sea very much, so I was in reflective mood.

The *Ramillies* was fitted with jamming equipment to interfere with the enemy's coastal radar, and it was Jim's job to switch this on. By D-Day the crew were ready for action. He recalls the journey across the Channel as uneventful.

Here am I, this little scion from New Zealand, I'm pacing the quarterdeck of a battleship, I've got nothing else to do. The whole blinking show is set up, the whole thing, the targets identified, the guns are ready. The radar sets are ready, the jamming equipment's all ready to be switched on. We're not there yet. It's evening and I'm pacing up and down the quarterdeck and I'm simply reflecting. This jolly battleship is so stable that I hardly feel a thing. I'm not talking about glory or courage at this juncture. I just know that my ship is heading across the Channel, that I'm responsible for the radar gear, everything's in place and it is a big occasion, and it's nice to be part of it. We got into position in the evening.

When Captain Middleton announced that the *Ramillies* was at last heading for Normandy, he added an unusual rider. In 1940 the ship had docked in Wellington Harbour before escorting the First Echelon of New Zealand troops to World War Two. During the visit, the Ngati Poneke Maori Association entertained the ship's company and presented a piupiu made by Pirihia Heketa. At the time of the presentation the *Ramillies* was blessed – as long as the captain wore the piupiu whenever the ship was in danger, no harm would come to it or to any member of the crew. When the first detachment of troops pulled away from shore, everyone sang 'Po Atarau' / 'Now is the Hour' in Maori and English. This became the ship's song.

Jim Pollok remembers the words of Captain Middleton as he announced the *Ramillies* was to set sail for its position off the Normandy coast.

It's then he used the famous words, 'And I shall be wearing the Maori skirt'. The reason he says that is this is the greatest morale-booster on the ship, this is going to protect the whole ship's company and the ship from any harm, and it's quite remarkable.

Did you know anything about it before he said that?

No, I didn't know a thing about the Maori skirt. I don't know what I thought. I suppose I must have thought it was a bit odd. It meant a whole lot to the crew, primarily in the lower deck. The ship had been to Madagascar before, and there's a story about the Maori skirt and the Madagascar campaign. That was before I joined the ship. The ship actually got torpedoed then and they said that was because the captain wasn't wearing the Maori skirt. But it didn't sink, and that was because the Maori skirt was locked up in his cabin. And each draft of seamen coming on board the ship sooner or later all heard something about the Maori skirt and – 'What on earth is this Maori skirt?' – 'Oh, that's what the skipper wears, and when the skipper wears it, we're alright.' And Captain Middleton was brave enough to wrap it around his loins when he went up to the bridge at action stations on D-Day.

Jim did not see Captain Middleton wear the piupiu, but a friend who was a Royal Marine bugler on the *Ramillies* has sent him a signed affidavit saying that he saw the captain wearing it on D-Day.

> There's always a Royal Marine bugler on the bridge of a battleship to sound off the various calls which are made from the bridge to the ship's company – it's really a relic of sailing days before you had modern means of communication. So he's up there, and he's there when Captain Middleton comes up on the bridge and he's wearing the Maori skirt alright. It's quite extraordinary because Captain Middleton was all of six foot tall and he wore a monocle. So he was a sort of archetype, you know, English naval officer and gentleman. He was quite pukkah, he sensed all this stuff about the Maori skirt – and after all, we didn't know what we were in for, really. We knew there was a dangerous coast for sure, and anything could happen to the ship. The batteries could aim at a ship, but also Le Havre was there and all these E-boats and U-boats and submarines and things. I mean it wasn't exactly a pleasant location. The thing is that this ship came through two world wars unscathed. A lucky and a happy ship.

The *Ramillies* did escape harm on D-Day, unlike a vessel close by. Torpedoes from E-boats hit a nearby Norwegian destroyer, the *Svenner*, which sank with the loss of 34 lives.

> There's a sudden commotion and someone pokes his head around the door and says there's a ship sunk, so I go out and then see with my own eyes the *Svenner*, broken in two and sinking just 100 or 200 yards away from the *Ramillies*. Just sank before your eyes. And that was perhaps the most dramatic D-Day moment for me. It was just part of the drama of the day. There's nothing you can do about it. You say, 'It's copped it.' You know there are men in the water, even if you don't see them.

The day after D-Day the *Ramillies* returned to Portsmouth to take on more ammunition, and then sailed back to Normandy. The enemy coastal batteries were not the only targets. The battleship was also instructed to support the attack on the town of Caen, some kilometres inland from Sword Beach. The bombardment of the city and its rail marshalling yards was relentless.

The *Ramillies* became the major bombarding battleship, I'm sorry to say wreaking havoc on the city of Caen, because the Germans were using that as a hinge, a point of resistance for the whole of their campaign. It was obviously within range of the ship. They reckon these 15-inch missiles weighed close on a ton each, and you're hurling them through the air. The talk on the ship was simply that we were doing our stuff, banging them off, to the extent that after about ten days or so the captain posted a signal which I've always remembered – and the Royal Navy has its own special language which it conjures up particularly when it sends signals, and so this read, and I can see this on the noticeboard, '*Ramillies* to Admiralty. My thousandth round has just rung a merry chime on Caen'. So that's the language used in warfare. And back comes the signal from Admiralty to *Ramillies*, 'Well done, *Ramillies*'.

I've subsequently reflected on what those thousand rounds of 15-inch high-explosive meant for Caen. It depends how you view it. If you're not particularly warlike, you realise you've wreaked an awful lot of destruction. I don't exactly enjoy the captain's signal. I can understand how it had come to be written. When I see the destruction of warfare I don't enjoy it, and this is just the physical destruction, but along with that goes the human obliteration, there is no other word for it.

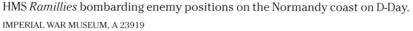

HMS *Ramillies* bombarding enemy positions on the Normandy coast on D-Day.
IMPERIAL WAR MUSEUM, A 23919

Jim Pollok's association with his old ship and its piupiu did not end with the war. In 1993, at a reunion of the HMS *Ramillies* Association in England, he learnt that the piupiu had been lost when the ship was broken up. As the only New Zealander present, he was asked to find a replacement. Back home, he made contact with the Ngati Poneke Maori Association and met Riria Utiku who, with her late husband, Rangi Katakua Utiku, had been in the performing party on the *Ramillies* in Wellington in 1940 when the piupiu was presented to the ship. Riria still had the piupiu that Rangi had worn on that occasion and generously offered it as a gift to the *Ramillies* Association. Ngati Poneke held a ceremony and church service and the replacement piupiu was blessed before Jim took it to England, where it is now on permanent display in the Royal Marines' Museum at Southsea. Here Geordie Gavin, the president of the HMS *Ramillies* Association in 1994, holds the replacement piupiu at a special dinner in Portsmouth. JIM POLLOK COLLECTION

From the battle for Normandy, the *Ramillies* was sent to the south of France to support a further landing which faced no real opposition.

In October 1944, after four years at sea, Jim Pollok was given leave to return to New Zealand. From the day he left the *Ramillies* he missed the ship and his friends among the crew. After a couple of months at home, he joined HMS *Indefatigable* in the Pacific. He was on the ship when it sailed into Tokyo Bay after the Japanese surrender.

After the war Jim completed his PhD and became a soil scientist at Massey University. In 1975 he married Fay Fairbrother, a schoolteacher. He reflects with

Jim Pollok, 2004. ALISON PARR

satisfaction on the contribution he was able to make on the *Ramillies* at the time
of the Normandy invasion.

> I've been digging up the records. I found this flimsy, which is a sort of a
> piece of paper the captain has to write whenever someone leaves the ship.
> Dated 17 October 1944:

>> *This is to certify that J A Pollok has served as Lieutenant Special Branch
>> Royal New Zealand Navy Volunteer Reserve under my command from
>> the 23rd day of August 1943 to the 27th day of September 1944, during
>> which period he has conducted himself with zeal, ability and to my entire
>> satisfaction. By his personal application he has brought the radar equipment
>> to a high pitch of efficiency and operational value. Determined to surmount
>> all difficulties. Signed G B Middleton, Captain, HMS* Ramillies.

> So I evidently had something to do with bringing the radar equipment to
> a high pitch of efficiency and operational value. But it was all done by an
> amateur!

John Morris, 1942. JOHN MORRIS COLLECTION

John Morris

FLIGHT LIEUTENANT, 75 (NZ) SQUADRON AND 15 SQUADRON,
BOMBER COMMAND, RAF

*We'd finally done it, got onto Europe. Then everybody began to
realise things were not going as well as they should do. We were
stuck there for a long time.*

JOHN MORRIS WAS A RELUCTANT BOMBER PILOT. HE WOULD HAVE PREFERRED TO
fly a fighter plane – as he saw it, with more freedom and no responsibility for
a crew. But the RAF had other ideas, and after training he was posted to 75 (NZ)
Squadron as flying officer on Lancaster bombers. He was 21.

John was born in Cambridge in 1923 and was working for the State Advances
Corporation when war was declared. After initial training in New Zealand, he
spent seven months in Canada, graduated as a potential fighter pilot and was commissioned in June 1943. While travelling on the *Mauretania* from New Zealand to
Canada he had met his first Germans, prisoners of war en route to POW camps.

> They were kept down in the bowels of the ship, they never appeared on
> the deck, but we got on famously with these blokes. A friend and I went
> down, I don't know what excuse we used, but we went down there a bit.
> These chaps taught us how to do the German dancing where you slap your
> thighs and that sort of thing. Amazing, stupid carry-on but it was a good
> experience from my point of view inasmuch as they were the first Germans
> I'd ever met and they were normal human beings, young fellows like us. It
> made me think about it all.

At the time John and his fellow aircrew arrived in England, bombing raids over
Germany were intense and it was not uncommon for the RAF to lose more than 30
bombers a night. They needed replacement bomber pilots, and John was drafted

for training. Pilots were able to select their crew and John first chose his navigator, Jim Wilkinson from Wellington.

> Amidst the group of navigators I saw a New Zealand officer and I thought, by gosh he will do me, so I suggested that he come in my crew and he seemed to be happy enough about that. We hit it off right from the start because we both had the same sort of ideas.

John and Jim chose the rest of their crew, and at the time of D-Day the men were in a Heavy Conversion Unit at Wratting Common in southern England, training to fly Stirlings. They knew that something big was happening.

> You couldn't help but be aware of the build-up. There were all these Americans everywhere, and all their gear and their trucks and tanks and God knows what, all parked around the place. There was a big concentration of Dakota aeroplanes near us, and we knew what they were. I can remember these things flying over us. A lot of them were towing gliders and that stream went on for what seemed like hours at night, all these aircraft heading off south, and then the next morning we heard on the news that it was all on. I knew very well that the people would be in dire trouble. I couldn't understand how they were going to get ashore without being slaughtered. I was in awe of what was happening.
>
> We were very much concerned with our own progress in training and learning to survive. That was the main thing. You couldn't help but realise the game was pretty close, and then bang off it went. Everybody was relieved – we'd finally done it, got onto Europe. Then everybody began to realise things were not going as well as they should do. We were stuck there for a long time.

After further training John and his crew were finally posted to 75 Squadron in July 1944, based at Mepal in Cambridgeshire. The morning after his arrival, John was told to report for briefing and informed that he was going to fly that night with a crew captained by Noel Stokes from Christchurch. The operation was to Stuttgart. He would fly as 'second dickey' or second pilot – a convention with newly trained pilots before they flew operationally with their own crew for the first time.

> We took off in the late afternoon. It was a really wonderful experience. I found that really exciting. I used to love that noise, the four Merlin engines starting up and giving an immense sense of power and strength. When

you multiply that by 30 aeroplanes, we all start up, we start taxiing towards the end of the runway, we're all nose to tail and all these engines ticking away, making this wonderful sound that they do, and then off they all go and they're throbbing power. Everything vibrates like mad in the aeroplane when you apply full power.

We were flying in the cloud, and hadn't been flying for all that long when I became aware of cannon shells going between my legs, under my legs and feet, and at the same time a whole shower of sparks and banging going on on the left-hand side. A German fighter had come up right behind us and then fired a long burst, and the rear gunner was killed and the aeroplane was badly damaged. The tail unit must have been badly damaged because the aeroplane was almost uncontrollable.

At this stage, one engine was on fire with flames streaming out behind it, and there was burning inside the aircraft. Noel Stokes dropped the bombs to make the aircraft easier to control, but, even with John Morris's strenuous assistance, was unable to keep it in the air. As it headed for the ground, Stokes gave the order to abandon the plane and the five crew who were alive got away. When John jumped, seconds before the plane crashed, Stokes was the only one left alive inside.

As soon as I was out of the aircraft and the aircraft went down, it blew up below me. So my first impression was that I was going up amidst all the debris from the aeroplane and the heat. Poor old Noel Stokes didn't have a chance. The plane went up with a whoof when it hit the ground. Even though it didn't have any bombs on it, it had a full fuel load and that was pretty tremendous. I was going upwards with a whole lot of debris with me and then I drifted away – I suppose at least one field away from the wreckage when I landed, where it was all burning. I dumped my parachute and Mae West [life jacket] and took off. I was burned in a way that, when a stove bursts you get a flash, that's all I got. It wasn't bad at all. My skin came off on my hands and my face.

Can you remember at all what was going through your mind?

Great relief at being alive. Being sad at the fact that poor old Stokes had had it. There was no doubt about that. I'd only known him for a few hours but I thought he was a really good bloke. Sad.

It became a very black night, a very dark night, and I had difficulty finding out where I was. I was in farmland. A lot of wheat had been cut and put in stooks. I had a map, an escape map made of silk, but I had to find out where I was and I came to a crossroads, and I can remember climbing up the signpost on the crossroads and feeling the names in French, trying to work out what they were. I established that one of the places was Dangeau, like danger, so I thought, that's appropriate, I won't go there. When I was floating down in my parachute, I could hear people talking and people running and that sort of thing and didn't know whether they were Frenchmen or Germans or what, so I was keen to get away from the area. I was very fit in those days and I must have run for bloody miles, actually. But I was pretty scared about the whole business.

How far did you run, how long had it been when you stopped running?

I suppose through to daylight to get myself hidden before it got light. It was one o'clock when I hit the ground, probably.

So where did you find to hide when daylight was coming?

I went into a wood and discovered a little hut. I made myself comfortable there. I was more frightened than exhausted, I think. A farmer came along and I told him what I was about. He came back and brought me some scruffy old clothes and took my air force uniform and made me look like a Frenchman.

These people were very brave in even acknowledging us and not turning us in. They were very brave. And they put themselves out. That young fellow passed me on to the schoolmaster in the nearby village, who could speak English, which was a big help because my French was hopeless. The schoolmaster was a great chap. They gave me a breakfast meal and a glass of wine, very watery wine which they drank all the time. But bearing in mind that they were all rationed, they didn't have much themselves. The fact that they so willingly shared the food, it was great. Wonderful people. They didn't make a song and dance about it. What they did do, which I found very embarrassing on more than one occasion, was at the drop of a hat they would all gather together and sing the 'Marseillaise', sort of cheering one another up I suppose. But they expected me to sing it and of course I didn't know it, hum the tune but the words, never, it was very embarrassing.

The schoolmaster passed me on to this house which was part of a shop, and this was the home of the Vouzelauds. They're very well known in that

Local people near Yèvres, France, examine the remains of the crashed Lancaster from which John Morris had bailed out, July 1944. The pilot, Lieutenant Noel Stokes of Christchurch, was killed in the crash. SERVICE DÉPARTEMENTAL DE L'EURE-ET-LOIR DE L'OFFICE NATIONAL DES ANCIENS COMBATTANTS ET VICTIMES DE GUERRE

part of France as manufacturers of sporting ammunition and guns. The Germans, to my surprise, allowed them to operate. I think they must have done bikes and things like that also. They had a workshop out the back and Maurice, the master of the house, had been in England, he'd been to one of the famous gunsmiths in London when he was a youngster and done part of an apprenticeship there, so he spoke good English and was in fact the head of the Resistance in the area. I stayed there one night.

Maurice's wife, Lucienne, was a very strong person. She said she didn't speak English, but in fact she did. She was a very able person, very strong personality, and she had these two little boys and yet she was still prepared to take tremendous risks for the likes of me. And I discovered after the war that she had had other airmen through her house, mostly Americans, and been in grave danger all the time. But she survived.

I remember making one of the biggest gaffes in my life in that house. With my limited French and my own stupidity I made a comment about the food that was served up to me. I remember it was pumpkin or something like that and I said, 'In our country we use this for pig food.' Oh God, I've never forgiven myself. Anyway that's the kind of thanks that they got. I think they were a bit horrified.

I was upstairs in part of this house and must have left the door open, and these kids saw me and had everybody immediately worried because they might say something at school, so I was shifted out of there pretty quickly.

The two of us, me and Lucienne, got on our bikes, she'd got two bikes and she was taking me on to somebody else. I remember I had an old pair of navy blue pants, flared sort of like sailors' pants, and some sort of check shirt, really old clothes and a pair of worn-out tan shoes. They'd taken my flying boots, which would have been a dead giveaway, but I suppose I looked like a local boy.

We were riding on the road and came round a corner and here are a whole lot of German soldiers right across the road, and they were obviously digging defences or doing something like that. Well it was too late to turn round, they were just around the corner, and quick as look she fell off her bike. She fell off deliberately, and fell so that she got grazed, and all these young German soldiers rushed to help her, because she was a really attractive young woman, and I just rode on, so nobody sort of noticed me. After a while, when I got about 100 yards up the road, I turned round and I thought, God I'd better go back, and she was lying on the ground at this stage and I could see her. She saw me, she saw what I was doing, and as soon as she saw me starting to come back she jumped up and made a sudden recovery and jumped on her bike to join me, and off we went. We were so lucky.

And the Germans just let her go?

Yeah. They were all astonished, I suppose, but it's amazing what an attractive young woman can get away with.

Did Lucienne say anything to you when she caught up with you, after her faked fall?

Oh something to the effect, 'Don't be a bloody idiot and go back there.' You know, 'You were supposed to keep going!' She took me to the local doctor, called Bietrix, and his wife was a very sophisticated Frenchwoman, not much older than I was. But boy, she was really something. They had a very nice place. I stayed there only for – it might have been one night, and then he took me in a car, because he was a doctor he was able to drive a Citroën round. He took me to Freteval Forest.

Did you have to hide in the car at all?

No, and I found this very hard to face. I expected Germans around every corner, but they weren't. We drove without incident.

Freteval Forest was a wooded area used by the French Resistance as a staging camp for many Allied airmen. John stayed there for about two weeks. Several of the local people who provided food to the men in Freteval were caught and never returned from concentration camps.

> These poor French people, at great risk to themselves, were bringing in stuff. It was not enough, we were all short of food and they had very little. They could get farm produce and bring that sort of thing to us, but nothing fancy at all and not enough – occasionally a bit of black bread and things like turnips, and a little bit of meat occasionally that you could make a stew with. But very little.
>
> I decided to walk toward the Allied lines, and a couple of others set off with me. The first place we hit was called Mondoubleau, and the people in this village were celebrating the fact that the Americans were just outside. And we got a really good feed that night, steak and eggs and chips. Wonderful food. And lots of liquor, and it was great. Proper Calvados, getting towards apple country I suppose. And they handed us over to some Americans who took us to one of their base places. They were running trucks back and forth with ammunition and stuff like that, and we went through St Lo to Cherbourg with them.

Back in London, John was reunited, at the New Zealand Forces Club, with his navigator, Jim Wilkinson, who had also been missing. He learnt that of his original crew only the two of them would resume flying. Two had been killed, one was a POW and one declined further operations.

John was posted to 15 Squadron RAF at Mildenhall and began flying again in November 1944 with Jim Wilkinson as his navigator. They flew fourteen operations with 15 Squadron, including raids on cities such as Cologne, Dortmund, Bonn and Nuremburg as well as strategic targets. Like some other bomber pilots, John Morris still feels distressed about the bombing of German cities. At the time, he tried not to think of German civilians – but he remembers one particular raid on the city of Trier on the Mosel River.

> It was horrifying. On that day, it was just before Christmas, December 21st, I was thinking of all the people with their Christmas trees getting ready. It was all snow-covered, beautiful. Dead clear, lovely clear day, not a cloud in the sky. And to think in that beautiful, pristine, virginal sort of setting you dropped these bloody awful great bombs on the people down there . . . it's awful really.

John Morris (left) and his navigator, Jim Wilkinson, in England in 1944, before their second experience of being shot down. JOHN MORRIS COLLECTION

On the night of 3 February 1945, the crew flew on an operation to Dortmund. They successfully bombed their target, but as they were turning to leave, they were caught in searchlights and soon had German fighters on their tail.

> This fighter was obviously following me and he let us have it, and it wasn't very long before we were on fire and in trouble. The gunners were killed when they first hit us, and then we struggled for a while and I could see that the engine, the whole wing was on fire, and I decided that it was time to go. So I gave the order to abandon aircraft – 'Abandon aircraft! Emergency! Jump. Jump!' And away they go.

Did you all bail out roughly around the same time in the same area?

> Quickly, one after the other, but I never saw any more of them. I landed fortunately in a field, no obstructions, there wasn't much wind which was lucky, but it was very dark and I hit the ground with a hell of a thump and unexpectedly. I thought I had plenty of time, but I was desperately cold. From my experiences of evading capture earlier on I had determined what I really needed always was a good knife, and I'd gone up to Sheffield and bought a knife, a really good one and had it honed like a razor. I always carried this in addition to the knife that was in my flying boot. I kept it in

A Lancaster bomber flying over Germany, 1944. JOHN MORRIS COLLECTION

my jacket, so the moment I landed I took my clothes off, most of them, cut the parachute up and wrapped the bits of silk on my body and then put my jacket back on. What I hadn't realised was that I was so cold I'd really cut my hand badly and I didn't know it. So there was blood all over the place and it looked as though I was hurt, whereas I really wasn't. Then I hid the remains of the parachute and took off.

Did you run again like the other time?

Not quite the same way, because the ground was very wet and soggy and a lot of snow around. And I got onto a road and I started walking. I'd got a rough indication from the stars where I should be walking, and in the Northern Hemisphere you've got the Pole star and it's much easier than it is down here to quickly establish where you are. I started walking along this road and almost straight away I met Germans. I couldn't speak German, so I grunted a greeting to these people and they seemed to accept it. It was dark and that threw them.

 Then I got off the road and went cross-country. Eventually I holed up and spent the next day hidden up in a clump of trees, and then I started walking. I got so close I could hear the British soldiers talking and I thought, by golly I reckon I can make it from here. And I stepped onto a big sheet of ice, which although it was pretty solid didn't support my weight, and it cracked and broke and I fell into this shallow water with a hell of a lot of noise and the German soldiers grabbed me. Fortunately didn't shoot me. They took me down into a concrete bunker that they were occupying overlooking this river. Being captured was a great disappointment.

I was still cold but these soldiers in this bunker included an officer. They had their eyes on the silk. They pretty quickly got my jacket off and took all the silk away. But then to my surprise, you get these surprises all the way along, the German officer gave me a sweater. He could see that I was dying of cold. He gave me this woollen hand-knitted sweater. Probably his wife had given it to him. I had it right through till the time I ceased to be a prisoner. I could tell that he was embarrassed by the fact that they were taking the silk off me. But it was good – human relationships, you know, it's not all bad.

From there I was taken to Mönchengladbach in Germany. There was a big air force establishment there and it was one of the few times that I was rough-handled. I was taken into this place in Mönchengladbach and there was a group of female air force people, Luftwaffe, equivalent of our WAAF, and they gave me a bad time. Very difficult. Beat me up and tried to humiliate me, not the sort of thing any man wants to happen.

Did it involve sexual taunts?

Yes, great fun. They were enjoying themselves. Half a dozen of them, I suppose. Just good clean fun, kicking and belting you, you know, just laughing and having a great old joke. I suppose I was in there for half a day.

Then I was taken off – how the clock swings back and forward, I'd met those awful people and felt any German was a dead loss, and then I was given a guard, a single German guard, a young man who was a university student actually, and he took me hundreds of miles. He saved my life and he did his job, couldn't have been more pleasant and cooperative, to make things as easy as he possibly could. Such a change. He took me by public transport to this place called Dulag Luft – the air force, Luftwaffe specialist interrogation centre – quite a long way away down south, mid-Germany.

When we arrived at the station at Dusseldorf there was a big air raid on and bombs were dropping round the station. We got out of the train as quickly as we could and he took me down into the bowels of the station, it was a very big railway station. When we got down . . . here were hundreds if not thousands of people down there sheltering from the bombing and all were bloody angry and upset, and when they saw me coming they wanted to get at me. This young German fellow, at great risk to himself, kept them off me. He cocked his gun and stood protectively in front of me and backed me into a corner and he protected me from there. If he hadn't done, I'd have been killed sure as eggs, they'd have thrown me into the fire probably, as they were known to do.

So you found yourself at Dulag Luft. Were you interrogated there?

Yes, but I discovered they knew more about 15 Squadron than I did. They just told me. I was a bit concerned there because they gave us a bit of treatment to soften us up a bit. No food, and they keep the lights on and all that sort of thing all night, and disturbing you all the time so that you couldn't sleep. But actually the interrogation was easy. It was obvious what was happening in the war by then.

It was while I was there at Dulag Luft I saw a fellow, American, calmly get up – he was sitting down leaning against the hut – and walk to the wire, stepped over the first warning wire and climbed steadily up the fence wires until he was shot. Bang. Gone. It sort of made the rest of us pause and think for a while.

In Dulag Luft John had met up again with his navigator, Jim Wilkinson, and they were taken together to Nuremburg. There they joined a column of thousands of other prisoners of war, ordered to begin a long march south to Munich.

I was very fortunate having Jim Wilkinson, particularly. We were very close. We had no food and very little in the way of clothing, and certainly no bedding. Jim somewhere found an old horse blanket. It was quite a big blanket, and so he rolled that up and put it round his neck and carried it the first day. I had somehow got hold of a needle and cotton and sewed it up and made a sleeping bag out of it, and two of us got into this sleeping bag because we could keep warm. We survived the first few nights because of that, I think.

That first day we became entangled with a couple of soldiers from the Norfolk Regiment who'd been prisoners since the beginning of the war. They took us under their wing really and showed us how to look after ourselves, which was very, very fortunate. They had a little burner that was made out of milk tins and things, and they could boil water up in a flash. Well, the first time we encountered this we were stopped across a railway line, and as soon as we had to halt they took their gear off and they were running around picking up little wee bits of coal off the railway line, and they brought this coal back, lit the burner and they had a pot going. One of them saw a chook. They caught that chook, they had the feathers off it and it was in the pot all cut up in little bits, in a flash. This scrawny chicken. And we had a bloody good meal. There was probably a few bits of puha or something in it as well – what we could gather around there. And all done with the guards around and all, and they didn't even see what was going on.

Other people would have been quite keen on having some too, wouldn't they?

Yes.

So how did you keep them away? What was the control like in that situation?

It was very dicey. But most of the people . . . they'd fall down and go to sleep. Anyway, that was the start of our education, and we got better and better at it as we moved on.

On the march the weather started off very bad, and Jim and I did everything to try and keep ourselves warm. He was a bit skinnier than me and he began to get very weak. We had one brush where he collapsed on the road, because he'd been weak and staggering. We'd drifted a bit to the tail of our particular column. He fell down and the Germans were kicking him and bashing him with their rifle butts to make him get up and walk, so I rushed back and they belted me. He saw me getting a hiding so he jumped up. He suddenly got new energy and it was really amazing, and we both scuttled back into the column. He'd seen what was likely to happen and he made a tremendous effort then to keep going. When these chaps started to collapse the Germans would just, Bang. If they fell – you know, old Jim got very close to getting a bullet. Somewhere, from in his body, he summoned some more energy that he didn't have before. Adrenalin, anger, I suppose it was in him that he sprang to life. He was pretty close to getting the treatment there.

We were desperately short of food. At that stage when Jim was so weak, it was obvious to anybody looking on that he was in a very bad way. I remember an old German woman coming out and gave me a big round loaf of bread, and that did wonders for Jim. If the guards had seen her they'd have shot her. There were other instances like that. If you walked close to the footpath, people would slip you an egg or something like that. Amazing.

Some of the things that happened illustrated how much they had to put

A column of POWs on a forced march in Germany like the one John Morris and Jim Wilkinson endured. These men have just sheltered in a ditch during an air raid. KIPPENBERGER MILITARY ARCHIVE & RESEARCH LIBRARY, ARMY MUSEUM, WAIOURU, DA-12571

up with, those people. For instance, on one night we entered a little town which I've subsequently been to, where there's a beautiful church. It's got world-famous decorations in it. Now, it was dark when we got there and they herded us into this church, thousands of us it seemed. There was hardly room to lie down on the floor or on the pews, and most of us, even though we weren't getting food very much, had to go to the toilet. There were no toilets in the church, of course, so we were all directed to use the front steps. When we got up the next morning it was the most ghastly filthy thing you could imagine, and we were marched on, of course, we weren't concerned with it any more. But those local people would have to clean up the mess. Terrible.

Throughout that whole time the Germans were totally disorganised. There were American fighters, Thunderbolts and Mustangs and things buzzing around all the time, and anything that moved was likely to get shot up. And we were terrified that we would get shot up when we were marching on the road.

It took about ten days for the column to march south from Nuremburg to Munich. From there, they were taken to a huge POW camp, Stalag VIIA, near Moosburg. Originally established to hold 10,000 men, by the end of the war it housed ten times that number. John and Jim were in the camp for about two months. Early on, they decided to swap identities with a couple of New Zealand soldiers.

As an officer you had no chance of getting out, but as a private soldier you would be taken out on work parties, and we figured that this would give us a better chance. So we became two privates in the New Zealand army. They became air force officers. They had an idea in their head that they'd be better looked after, which was totally wrong, of course. We just changed the identity discs. So we did that switch and the result was that they disappeared off into the officers' compound and were stuck in an encampment with no facilities at all. Through the wire beside us were the Russians. Now the Russians were treated like second-grade animals. We got badly treated enough inasmuch that we got one Dixie, one big cup of soup a day and that was our lot, and if it had anything in it you'd be lucky, it was normally thin gruel, just very little. But the Russians got nothing. They were dying like flies. You could see bodies lying. They had typhus in there. There were huge numbers of these people and what we were worried about was that we'd get typhus. You knew enough to know that you'd get typhus from lice, and the big thing is to keep yourself clean as you possibly can. I can see Jim standing there in the snow, there was snow on the ground, and no clothes on, stark naked, shaving his genitals with a blunt razor. A very, very unpleasant experience, but it shows how determined we were not to succumb to typhus if we could avoid it. The two of us claimed as our own the very corner of the compound. We didn't want to have anybody near us, keep away from these people who might have typhus or lice.

Mostly you were concerned with trying to find something to eat or talking about escaping – that sort of thing. We seemed to stay in that corner to stake our claim there. It depended on who else was around. We had done this switch of identities to facilitate our getting out, but we were never taken out on a work party so that came to nothing.

Can you remember what the camp smelt like?

Ghastly, because it was all these Russians in the next compound, dying and not being disposed of quickly. It was awful. I don't think the Germans did anything for them. They all seemed to be in terror of the war ending and them being taken back into the communist fold, because they had been told that prisoners would be shot. So they were in a hell of a dilemma, those poor fellows.

I lost a lot of weight, but other than that I was in pretty good nick. It's a funny thing, when you're starving your whole mind seems to, well from my experience, focus on rectifying that situation. We never talked about sex or anything else except food. If we were talking about what we'd do when the war was over or when we got out of this situation, I can remember

John Morris, 2005. ALISON PARR

stating that my plan was to have a steak dinner while sitting on a toilet in a tiled bathroom. Cleanliness and good food were the thing. Booze and sex and that sort of thing were way down the list.

We could hear the guns for days before the Americans actually arrived, and then suddenly there was a helluva roar and old Patton himself arrived at the gates of our camp, standing in the turret of a tank. He was the first guy I saw. It was wonderful. They just drove in over the gates, just smashed the thing down. Rolled over the top and then he disappeared off almost straight away, then some other American tanks came in. But then the Americans, with all the will in the world, they couldn't cope with the situation. It's not as though they then started handing out the rations or anything, it took some while for them to bring us some food. Some people went into the town. They walked out. A lot of people disappeared. I wanted to stay there until I was going to be taken to an airfield and flown out.

General Patton arrived at the camp on 29 April 1945. John and Jim remained there for a further two or three days before they were taken by Americans to an airfield and flown to Brussels and thence to England.

After his return to New Zealand, John Morris joined the regular army, in which he served until 1978. He married Pamela Murray in 1951 and they have three sons.

Lucienne and Maurice Vouzelaud in 1943. LUCIENNE VOUZELAUD COLLECTION

Lucienne Vouzelaud

RESISTANCE WORKER, BROU, FRANCE

We didn't think about it at all, and we believed it had to be done,
that's all. We could not let the Germans take them.

MAURICE AND LUCIENNE VOUZELAUD WERE AMONG THE THOUSANDS OF FRENCH men and women who worked for the Resistance during the German occupation of their country in the Second World War. Defying the dangers, they gave shelter and helped to safety thirteen Allied airmen from the United Kingdom and America. After the war they were recognised by the government of the United States for their courage.

In the first year of the war Maurice had been mobilised to serve with the French navy in the North Sea. He saw many ships being blown up by enemy mines, was captured and spent time as a POW. He was deeply disturbed by these experiences and felt badly towards the Germans. Invalided out of service after recovering from tuberculosis, he returned to his wife and two young sons in Brou, a small town near Chartres. In 1942 he was approached to join the Resistance and accepted without hesitation. Lucienne was immediately involved too.

> Well, I followed him, of course. I agreed. We did not know what our joining involved. We had to find out. But we accepted straight away. There were all sorts. People who wanted to take part, who wanted to help, who wanted to support each other. Well, we were in the pack. We did not speak of politics, not at all. In any case, most of the people who had joined were not interested in politics. They wanted to do something, that's all.

Lucienne and Maurice were part of the Comète Line – one of the chains of Resistance workers in France. Networks of civilians kept the lines functioning, passing Allied airmen on to others in the chain, and to eventual safety.

A French Resistance worker sets an explosive charge on a railway line, one of thousands of acts of sabotage against the German occupiers carried out by members of the Resistance. Their other main activities were gathering intelligence and helping Allied airmen and prisoners of war escape the country. An estimated 500,000 French men and women worked for the Resistance from June 1940 until the end of the war. The risks were great. More than 90,000 resisters were killed, tortured or deported by the Germans.

IMPERIAL WAR MUSEUM, HU 56936

I must say that sometimes the escape networks worked very quickly, especially at the beginning. But afterwards it could all break down very easily, you only needed to make one wrong move. At that point everything's broken off! Nobody wants to know you. It's up to you to find another network, and it's not easy. One day I made a wrong move and nobody wants to know you any more. We managed to find another link. But it took a few days, of course. It wasn't easy. We had to search in Paris among our connections, among our acquaintances, and in the end we managed to find a new link. Before the war, we were renting an apartment in Paris. We used to go there for our business. We had very reliable friends there. It was with them that we found another link.

The Resistance workers who were most closely involved with the Vouzelauds were Dr Pierre Bietrix and his wife, who lived in a nearby town.

We used to work in complete accord with them, and when they had a problem they would refer to us and we would refer to them, so it was Madame Bietrix who took them. They had a link that came from Belgium, the Comète, she was Belgian, Madame Bietrix. For me, the first stop was Bietrix, and I knew that after Bietrix they went directly to Freteval [a forest camp where Allied escapees were sheltered]. Freteval was when there was no more communication. It was right at the end of the war, when there were no more trains. After being bombed, destroying bridges and so on, there was no more communication, there were no more trains. Otherwise the Resistance line used to run to Paris. The first ones used to run very well with Comète.

How were the airmen? Were they afraid?

They had complete trust in us, complete confidence. When they bailed out we would grab them, we would dress them like tramps and then we would take them there with us. Because you had to take their clothes off, they had to leave their uniform as soon as they bailed out because otherwise you would not be able to walk around with them. It was the first thing to do. They had no idea where they were, and then we grabbed them. As soon as we knew there was trouble we were off. But you had to act very quickly and most of all, not leave them in their uniform.

You had two young children at the time. Did you worry about them?

Well, we did not think about it. We could not see what else we could have done. We didn't think about it at all, and we believed it had to be done, that's all. We could not let the Germans take them. So it had to be done, in our eyes at least it had to be done.

But your life and your children's lives could have been in danger.

Yes, of course. But we thought about it afterwards, when the war ended, because everybody told us. But at the time, if you don't do anything . . . there were enough cowards, people who were chicken, like that. You know, it's true, you have to take risks. The lads we were mixing with, they were very reliable lads – you have to know who you are dealing with.

During the occupation, while you were in the Resistance, did you know what happened to the Resistance fighters who were caught?

Oh yes! We knew that, there had already been about fifteen people shot in the area, at Maintenon, and everywhere, the Sadorge. . . . They were caught, shot. Maybe because it was part of the risk, we found it even more exciting to take the risk. My husband and I, we took action, did what we could, as quickly as possible, but we were happy to do it. And that's all I can say. We were happy. We would have been jealous if others had done it instead of us!

Was there ever a time when you were truly afraid?

Maybe, but I don't remember anymore. You have to know that the local area was very, very discreet. People were very discreet. There were a few you could not trust . . . we knew about them. My husband used to know them in the Resistance and he knew those that could not be trusted in the local area, because sometimes those people were put in the hot seat in order to be shot, to be got rid of by the Resistance. And my husband was always against it, because he said you only had to keep a close eye on them. But if there had been any arrests, they would have been bumped off, that's for sure. My husband used to say, 'After the war they will be judged. After the war they will be judged. But for now we don't move, no fuss. We must not attract attention.'

How did you manage to stop your children from telling that there were pilots in the house – like John Morris?

Lucienne Vouzelaud on her bicycle in the French countryside, 1940s. LUCIENNE VOUZELAUD COLLECTION

Well, the children had seen them and they did not tell us till after the war. They only told us after the war that they saw them.

It was not only the children who could have seen the Vouzelauds' 'guests'. At the same time as the family was sheltering Allied airmen, the German army was requisitioning rooms in French homes. The Vouzelauds' house, which Lucienne Vouzelaud still lives in today, has two small wings on either side of an internal courtyard – and there were times when Germans were in one wing and Allied airmen in the other. Even with this pressure, Maurice and Lucienne Vouzelaud remained calm.

> Well, we used to keep watch. There were two flights of stairs at the time, one for the staff entrance – because at the time we had a few staff at home – and the general stairs, so that the Germans could come down using the servants' staircase. But if we heard any noise we kept quiet anyway. We were careful. We were very careful and I must say that local people, apart from a few, were very discreet. Even if they knew, they did not say anything. They kept quiet, and there must have been some of them who suspected something.

At the time the Vouzelauds were helping Allied airmen, French families were living on very lean rations, even without the burden of extra mouths to fill. Years of war had depleted food stocks.

> Food supply was very, very difficult, especially in the towns, because for us in the country we used to kill animals, clandestinely. It was like a Mafia. We used Mafia ways in the Resistance. We were real Mafiosos. We used to make false identity cards, we made ration cards, we took pictures of the airmen to make identity cards for them, we affixed the seal of the Préfecture. But it was like a Mafia.

> *How did you manage to feed those airmen as well as everybody else?*

> Generally, we used to manage. You know, in the country we didn't have everything. We had no coffee, we had no chocolate, we did not have things like that, we did not have oil, nothing like that. But together we used to make fake soap. We managed. We ground on.

More than 60 years later, Lucienne Vouzelaud remembers the events that brought the young New Zealand pilot John Morris to her home.

After the war John Morris and the Vouzelauds remained in contact. Here he is reunited with his Resistance friends at an official function in France, 1963. Left to right: Madame Bietrix, John Morris, Madame Lucienne Vouzelaud, Monsieur Maurice Vouzelaud, Dr Pierre Bietrix.

Somebody told us that a plane had crashed at Yèvres, so we started to make enquiries about where the survivors went and there were two of them staying with a farmer. I only learned about it later. But these people, they didn't make any fuss. They looked after them.

How did John Morris get to your house?

We were told that there was one in Dangeau, staying with the Dangeau primary schoolteacher, who had just arrived. They had already had time to give him civilian clothes. But they did not know what to do after that, so we had been told about it. My husband went to get him and then he brought him here. Well, at that time the relay to go to Freteval was at Bietrix's, the famous Bietrix. So he came to us. He was very young, John Morris, he was so young, so young. But lively, happy, ready for anything. So he stayed with us, not for long, a day or two perhaps, I do not remember any more. After that we told Bietrix that we had an airman with us. He told us, 'Bring him and I will evacuate him to Freteval'. So it was me who took him on a bicycle. I know we were singing, all the way on the road on our bicycles. We were singing, 'It's a long way to Tipperary', and my sister-in-law, who was very lively, she was with us as well. She was saying, 'Oh, you're going

Lucienne Vouzelaud, 2005.

to get us into trouble with your silliness.' We didn't worry. We thought it was funny. We came across some Germans – it did happen sometimes . . . I fell off my bicycle, yes it's true.

After delivering John Morris to the next stage of the Resistance network, Lucienne Vouzelaud remained concerned about him. When the war ended she wrote to his mother and made enquiries about him. The connection re-formed then has lasted for the many decades since. In the 1960s the Vouzelauds, Bietrixs, and John Morris met again, in Paris. They remain in touch with each other. Madame Vouzelaud still regards her Resistance work with humility.

Sixty years later I tell myself that at that time, it was normal to do what we were doing.

Did you and your husband consider yourselves brave, courageous?

Absolutely not! We did what we could do. People around us told us how brave we were. Maurice said after the war, 'I don't want to talk about it any more. It is finished. This is a new page.'

LUCIENNE VOUZELAUD   217

Les Munro, 1942. LES MUNRO COLLECTION

Les Munro DSO, DFC

SQUADRON LEADER, 97 AND 617 SQUADRONS,
BOMBER COMMAND, RAF

We had a job to do, come what may. If we were going to cop it, so
be it. I think I left New Zealand on that basis.

LES MUNRO WAS BORN IN GISBORNE IN 1919 AND GREW UP ON A SHEEP STATION
during the 'slump'. Life was tough for his parents, and he has particular admiration for his hardworking mother and his father, a station shepherd. After high school Les went to work on the land himself, on dairy and sheep farms in the Gisborne district.

At the outbreak of the Second World War he felt it was his 'natural duty to go and help the old country'. Les chose to fly bombers and left for training in Canada at the end of September 1941. In February 1942 he headed for England for more training, and it was while he was with an Operational Training Unit at North Luffenham that he flew his first bombing raid to Europe.

> The target was Dusseldorf. I think it was exciting to the extent that you could see a town being bombed and the searchlights wavering in the sky. I can't say that I was excited. I think part of my nature was such that right through my operational career I accepted things. I didn't feel that I was in danger. Even to this day I feel that I was a fatalist. Well I am a fatalist anyway, but right through the war I felt, we've got a job to do, let's do it. I concentrated on flying the aircraft, concentrated on making sure the crew was doing their job. But right through I don't think I can say that I ever got excited – that I ever felt that things were going wrong.

Three nights later, setting out on his second raid, he experienced the first major incident in his flying career. His plane failed to climb after take-off and settled in a nearby field before bursting into flames.

> We all got out. As we came to a standstill, I looked out and I could see flames flickering up in one of the motors, and I said, 'Get out fairly quickly', and so we got out and tramped across the paddocks in the dark, and the plane was burning behind us and in sequence the bombs went up as a result of the fire. I was too busy trying to get the plane up in the air to get too scared about anything. In retrospect, I never had any fear that night. It wasn't as if we suddenly had hit something hard and crashed, it just settled down like a nice easy landing. That's the first evidence that I had that luck was on my side during the war.

In December 1942, 18 months after he began training, Les was posted to 97 Squadron, based at Woodhall Spa. There was only one occasion during the war that Les can recall feeling fear, and it was on his first operation with this squadron. The task was to lay mines on the French coast at the mouth of the Gironde River.

> When we arrived at the target area we were flying low, of course, to be able to drop mines, and we could see the coast and it looked dark and ominous, and for some reason I felt a twinge of fear, in that, are we in the right area? Are we suddenly going to be fired at? I felt a twinge of fear in that sense – 10–25 seconds. There was not a sign of a light anywhere, it was just dark, this dark mass of land, and it just looked foreboding. We went to another mining operation a couple of nights later and it didn't happen again, and I've always wondered why that happened. It was sort of something flowed through my body. I just felt uncomfortable. I just felt something's not right here. But I can't explain it beyond that. Something just hit me. The only time I really felt fear in all the operations I did. I put that out of my . . . I think I cast that aside. I didn't feel that I was any more immune to the danger of enemy attack than any of the others. I don't think I had a feeling of being tough about it. I think right through, my general summation of my attitude to our operations was one of fatalism. If I'm going to cop it I'm going to cop it. I had luck on my side once or twice. I think most of us that went through the war had that element of luck.

Four of the crew Les chose during training stayed with him for the rest of the war: his navigator Jock Rumbles, a Scotsman; his wireless operator Percy Pigeon, a Canadian; and his flight engineer and mid upper gunner, Frank Appleby and Bill Howarth, both Englishmen. They, along with the bomb aimer and rear gunner, were keen to begin operational flying.

> There was a great deal of satisfaction once we got to the squadron. At long last you were going to be able to do something for what you originally enlisted for. A sense of achievement that you'd come through all those many months of training and at last you were going to be in the position to put your training into practice. This was the ultimate. To be able to put into practice the objective of taking part in the operations and attacking Germany. I think I had a sense of achievement in reaching there, but then ahead of you was the unknown. What was bomber operations going to be like? And how difficult was it going to be? What sort of opposition are you going to meet from light flak and from night fighters, and all that sort of thing? I suppose in a way there was a certain amount of trepidation about what you were going to be faced with.

Officers of 97 Squadron outside their mess at the Petwood Hotel, Woodhall Spa, Lincolnshire, 1943. LES MUNRO COLLECTION

An aerial view of an Allied bombing raid in Germany. Smoke clouds mark the destruction of key rail bridges on a vital enemy supply route. IMPERIAL WAR MUSEUM, FRA 102256

Bomber Command planned operations to do as much damage as possible to towns and cities in Germany – among them Berlin, Cologne, Essen and Hamburg. Even though it was midwinter and weather conditions were often not good for flying, the bombers continued their raids. As Les recalls, their intention was 'keeping the German population awake and affecting morale'. At this time German cities were heavily defended, and even after a successful raid no crews could relax until they returned to base.

You still had to get down at the end of the day – at the end of your trip you had to make a successful landing in the dark. I think generally speaking there was a sense of relief when you hit the runway and you throttled back and you taxied to your dispersal point. The other point where I had a sense of relief was when we flew away from the target, when we finished the bombing run and you were leaving the heavily defended area behind. There was a sense of relief then, when you were out of range of the guns and the searchlights. And certainly if you hadn't been caught by searchlights and you got away there was a relief that you hadn't been caught – because once you were caught in the beam of a searchlight, other searchlights would focus on you and that's when there was a danger.

Once you are on your bombing run you're set, you've got to stay on that bombing run and abide by the direction of the bomb aimer. If you're suddenly caught in a searchlight, just too bad. Everything's lit up like daylight. I was very rarely caught. And sometimes of course the searchlights will be waving across the sky trying to pick up planes. It gives you a very uncomfortable feeling. Once a plane was caught in a searchlight, other searchlights would concentrate on them and they'd have three or four, maybe half a dozen searchlights concentrating on this particular plane.

On one of the last trips that we did to Berlin while I was on 97 Squadron, it was a big raid, probably 500 to 600 or 700 aircraft on the job, and by the time we reached it Berlin was just a mass of fires. There were bombs exploding and there were searchlights everywhere and we'd just nearly finished our bombing run out of Berlin, and our wireless op Percy Pigeon decided he'd come out and have a look, the first and only time he ever did it. Got out from his desk and walked into the cockpit. The navigator and the wireless op couldn't see what was going on because they were enclosed because they had lights on to work their equipment. And so he come out and had a look, and he looked out the cockpit window and he looked back at this mass of flame and flak bursts in the sky and he said, 'Jesus Christ! Have we come through that?' And it just shows you, what you can't see, you don't worry about. The first time he'd ever seen what was going on outside. I'll always remember that, his exclamation.

97 Squadron had its share of the notorious losses experienced in Bomber Command. During the Second World War 109 aircraft from the squadron were shot down – more than 760 men. It required a particular attitude to keep flying in the face of such attrition.

If you'd become friendly with certain of the aircrew and you got back from a raid and you found that they'd been shot down or they didn't come back, you'd feel a degree of sadness. If you didn't know them personally it was just a fact of life. Didn't get you upset. But even the ones that you were friendly with, you'd feel a degree of sadness but after a couple of days you put it out of your mind completely. It was

Flying officers rest in the grounds of the Petwood Hotel, Woodhall Spa, 1943. LES MUNRO COLLECTION

dangerous to become too emotional about it because then you'd become affected in your ability to handle further raids, further operations. If you started to feel emotional about it and started thinking about having lost so and so, then that would affect your ability to carry out an operation, you know, subjectively. You couldn't dwell on it. In my view, you couldn't let grief interfere with your general approach to all the jobs you had ahead of you. I think in certain people, certain air force personnel, it did affect them to the extent that, in some cases, I think they were taken off operations.

Did you ever have any ideas or thoughts about the people below when you were bombing?

No, you put that out of your mind – even today I, you know, I feel that the bombs from my aircraft probably killed women and children and there's probably no doubt about that in all the operations I did. But that was part of . . . that was just one of the down-sides of the war, and I've accepted that as one of the necessities of war. But during the operations, no. I think if you started to do that, if you'd been flying over and said, God, I don't want to drop these bombs on these people, you'd start to lose it. You're going to forget what you're doing, forget what you're up there for.

Les Munro flying his Lancaster while in 617 Squadron, 1943. LES MUNRO COLLECTION

In March 1943 volunteers with experience were called to form a special squadron for a particular operation. By this time Les and his crew had flown 21 operations with 97 Squadron and felt like the challenge of something new. They volunteered and became part of 617 Squadron, even though they had no idea what task they were going to be assigned.

What they had offered their services for was Operation Chastise – the bombing of dams in the Ruhr Valley, at the heart of German industrial production. 617 was to become the Dam Buster Squadron. Throughout training, the crews remained in the dark about the operation. They had six weeks to prepare themselves.

> All our flying training was based on low-level training, cross-country flying, low-level simulated attacks on the English dams at Derwent Water and Uppingham Reservoir and coming down the North Sea. Any bombing training that we did was also based on low-level bombing.

Local people in the areas where training was taking place became increasingly unsettled by the fast, low-flying aircraft – to the extent that approaches were made to the squadron to stop training there.

> We as individual crews weren't aware. The squadron commander, Gibson, had been informed that people were complaining, and somebody responded that this was something they'd have to put up with.

Low-level flying in the air force was taboo. It was a court-martial offence. The fact that we were able to indulge in authorised low-level flying was welcomed by the pilots. It was great and it was an exhilarating experience flying at low level, at only 50 feet, at treetop height. I've never heard of how other crew members felt about the fact that they were flying so low to the ground and having their lives in the hands of a pilot in the front of the plane. I've heard one crew member reported as saying that they had complete confidence in my ability and he reckoned I had nerves of steel. I'm not sure whether that's completely accurate as far as the other crew members were concerned. But to start with, of course, it's a question of judgement. A major problem insofar as low flying was concerned was over the fen country in south-east Lincolnshire. The fen country was inhabited by myriads of seagulls, and as you flew along at 50 feet or something, these would all take off in front of you, and this was a real hazard and I had one hit right in the middle of the windscreen and smashed right through between the flight engineer myself and hit, splattered on the bulkhead of the navigator's compartment. If that had hit me or my face I don't know what would have happened.

We progressed from daylight low flying cross-country to synthetic, to try and ease the change from daylight to night. We adopted a system of putting blue perspex screens round the cockpit and the pilot and the crews wearing yellow goggles, tinted goggles, and this simulated moonlight flying conditions. And after we did a few trips like that we went straight into flying low level in moonlight. One of the main problems we struck was over the water, over the lakes, in moonlight conditions, if there was haze. The horizon disappeared, and there were one or two crews that had near misses, losing the horizon and nearly flying into the water.

While we were training there was a lot of conjecture as to what our target was. There were all sorts of suggestions and quite a number of people thought it would be one of the German battleships. Only a few thought that it would the dams, but because we were on a very, very strict security, we were not to talk to anybody so it wasn't openly discussed at all. It wasn't until the afternoon of the raid itself that we walked into the ops room and saw the big maps and the tapes leading to the target, and I think that in general there was no real concern about the actual targets. It was the fact that we had to go through all the heavily defended area of Germany to get there at low level.

The Lancasters the squadron flew for the Dam Busters raid had been modified to carry new bouncing bombs, designed by Barnes Wallis and codenamed 'Upkeep'. The operation was to take place in moonlight and crews were briefed to fly at 60 feet for the entire operation – at more than 200 miles an hour.

> It was something new. It was something we hadn't experienced before. I don't think any of the aircrews had flown at low level on operations before. I don't remember, personally, being worried about what was going to happen. I'd done enough trips on 97 then to not worry. In fact I never worried. I was a fatalist – we had a job to do come what may, and that was our job. If we were going to cop it, so be it. I think I left New Zealand on that basis, that if I copped it so be it.

On the night of the 16 May 1943, nineteen planes took off for the Ruhr Valley. They flew in two waves, with Les in the second.

> We flew low right across the North Sea and turned round and came down and hit the Dutch coast at the island of Vlieland. I can remember flying across and seeing the sand dunes in front of me and having to raise the aircraft to go over them, and as we're going down the other side I was hit by a light flak emplacement. It opened up on us. We just heard a bang and it blew a great big hole in the midships. It severed all intercommunication electrical wiring and of course the intercom went dead, there was no way of conversing with any of the crew. I carried on on the existing route down into the Zuider Zee and circled, and I asked my wireless op to go back with messages – lifting our helmets aside and yelling in each other's ears, and said, 'Go back and see whether you can rectify the damage so we can at least talk to each other', and I circled around the Zuider Zee while he was doing that. He came back and said, 'No, there's no way of repairing the damage.' It was imperative at low level, and certainly at the dams itself – it was absolutely imperative that we were able to communicate with each other. So I made the decision to return home and then went back and landed with the Upkeep [bomb] on. Flying at low level it was absolutely essential that you were able to talk to each other. I don't believe I had an option.
>
> At the time I was not really disappointed. It was afterwards, in the mess when those of the crews that had come back were celebrating and getting stuck into the grog that I felt sort of uncomfortable with the fact that I was not able to say, well, I've been one of them . . . the night when they came back, and daylight broke and here was everybody getting stuck in and celebrating. But of course that celebration was tinged with the sadness that

Aircrew and WAAFs relax outside Scampton officers' mess after the Dams raid, May 1943.
LES MUNRO COLLECTION

eight crews didn't come back. That sort of dampened down enthusiasm a little bit. And yet at the same time I often say, well, maybe if I'd gone, I might have been one of those eight crews that never came back. So it may be the luck of the gods.

Guy Gibson, the commander of the squadron, was awarded a VC for his part in the raid. The heavy losses to the squadron were added to four months later in a bombing operation on the Dortmund–Ems Canal – out of eight Lancaster crews sent, only three returned.

Over the fourteen months following the Dam Busters raid, 617 Squadron developed a name for its specialist and precision bombing role, attacking arms and aero engine works factories in cities, ammunition dumps, and later in the war destroying V2 bomb sites.

We were completely divorced from the main force and, I suppose I shouldn't say it, but we believed ourselves to be a cut above the average as far as the main bomber squadrons were concerned. And I think we've always been regarded as an elite squadron in that sense. The success of the

Les Munro talking with King George VI, just after the Dams raid. LES MUNRO COLLECTION

squadron was much greater than another squadron would have achieved, but that was our role of course, and we trained for that particular role.

As D-Day approached, 617 Squadron had no idea what its role would be during the invasion. Towards the end of April crews were told that the squadron was to train for a special operation, but the men were given absolutely no details. There was a great deal of secrecy.

> All I knew was that we would take off and go up to the coast and do these navigational exercises, flying on continuous circuits on specified airspeed and rate of turn and that sort of thing.

When the squadron was told, eventually, that they would not be flying operationally on D-Day, most of the crews were unhappy – their expectations were for something different.

> We were anticipating that we'd have a vital role to play, but an attacking role. The day that the squadron was advised that for security reasons they

were taken off operations to train for a specific job there were quite a number of very disgruntled pilots, particularly, and crews who saw their role more as an attacking role. When we were told we were taken off ops, there was quite a bit of disappointment expressed.

In keeping with normal secrecy concerning targets, it was only the afternoon before D-Day that the squadron learnt that their role would be to create a crucial diversion away from the Normandy beaches.

Three lines of ships from the Royal Navy would approach the French coast at the decoy point and 617 Squadron would help to create the illusion of many more – an armada heading for France. To do this, the squadron's planes would fly precise circuit formations, backwards and forwards on a prescribed course, while dropping long strips of aluminium foil, called Window, out of their planes. The foil would distort German radar, forming the impression that there was a fleet of ships approaching France much further north than the invasion forces were actually planning to land.

Les Munro and his crew in 617 Squadron. LES MUNRO COLLECTION

Window was something that bomber crews were familiar with – they had used it on normal bombing operations to confound German radar.

> For this particular operation they produced the foil in different sizes and lengths and thicknesses, so that as you approached the French coast it was longer and heavier and as you went away you dropped it smaller and lighter, to create the image of the front of a convoy at the beginning and tailing off to distant ships.
> From the point of view of our overall operations this is probably the most important operation we carried out, principally because of the exact nature that we were required to fly. No deviation from course, no change in altitude. We had to fly absolutely to within seconds – an oblong circuit for two minutes and 30 seconds on the outward leg, and two minutes and 10 seconds on the return leg, with a 180-degree turn at each end that had to take exactly one minute. That was the exact nature of the requirements to fly, and the navigators had to be so detailed ensuring the advice to the pilot, 'Turn here, stop turning, turn there.' Then the crew . . . somebody had to be governing the timing. They had red and green lights in the fuselage next to the flare chute where crew members were putting the bundles down exactly on time, every four and a half seconds.

The squadron took off late on the night of 5 June, flying into dawn of D-Day. Only sixteen of the squadron's 36 aircraft took part, but nearly all the crews were involved.

> Almost the whole squadron, certainly, because every crew doubled up. There were two crews in each aircraft – because of the stress of flying, the stress of the pilots, the concentration required and the stress that would result from flying hour after hour. And after each hour they swapped crews. And also the exact nature of the crews in the fuselage dropping Window, ad infinitum, every four and a half seconds. So they had to have spells, crews had to be spelled. All the pilots and navigators and the people responsible for controlling the dropping of the tinfoil were all doubled up.
> Leonard Cheshire, the CO of the squadron, flew with me as second pilot. We shared the pilot's duties. I flew out, I did the first hour I think, then he did the second hour, and then at the end of the two hours, a second wave of eight aircraft came in and took over the same pattern. We returned to base. That was it.

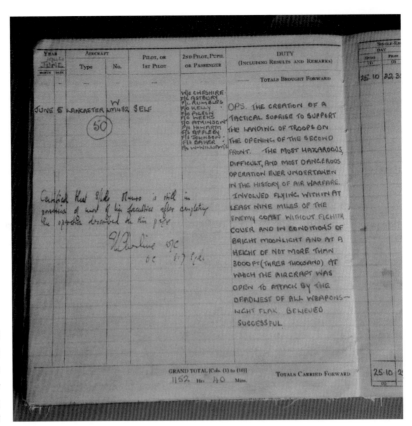

The page from Les Munro's logbook with his wry entry about the decoy mission flown by 617 Squadron on D-Day.
LES MUNRO COLLECTION

The only thing that got you was the concentration, the exact nature of flying, of maintaining your height without deviation, because once there was any deviation from the line that you were taking, or the height, it would have an effect on the Window and it would show up on the screen, and it would create suspicion in the German's mind that there was something not right here. So it was imperative that we avoided any departure from the given route or the height or the rate at which we dropped the Window.

I think gradually we overcame the disappointment of not having a bombing role. We had a very, very specific, very important role to play, but it was a very docile role. There was no enemy flak, there was no action, we weren't dropping bombs or anything. Even afterwards, this was demonstrated in my case, I went overboard in describing the operation, saying, 'The most hazardous operation in history of air warfare carried out in moonlight conditions at risk of light flak and attack by enemy fighters' – in the logbook, it's there, and on the page opposite my entry, Leonard Cheshire, the CO, wrote something along the lines that, 'I certify that

Squadron Leader Munro is still in possession of most of his faculties after having completed the operation described on this page'. It's quite amusing actually. It really was tongue in cheek.

The squadron later learnt that their operation was a success. The Germans had delayed diverting troops to Normandy as a result of the faked armada. Two days after D-Day the squadron returned to its attacking role. It bombed the strategically important Saumur railway tunnel in western France – the first use of Tallboys, deep-penetration bombs that were also known as 'Earthquake' bombs because of the shockwaves that resulted from their explosive force. A week later, on 14 June, Les led the Lancasters of 617 Squadron in an operation of which he is particularly proud.

> I led the squadron, all the Lancs in formation, in daylight, on Le Havre carrying 12,000 Tallboys, and that was quite an honour for me.

> *What was the aim of that operation?*

> Bombing the E-boat pens and the U-boat pens in Le Havre. The E-boat pens had been starting to worry the armada and it was decided to do a major attack on the pens at Le Havre, and one day later we went and bombed the E-boat pens at Boulogne. Both sites were heavily defended. According to reports we destroyed 133 E-boats – some of them were chucked up right onto land with the explosive force of the Tallboys. From then we went on to bombing the V2 sites.

These two raids stand out for Les as major contributions to the D-Day operation and the advance of the Allies.

In the main bomber force 30 trips were recognised as comprising a 'tour' of operations. The convention was that, after that, pilots were usually taken off operations for a compulsory break and given a training job. By July 1944 Les had done 58 trips without a break. It was decided his crew had done enough. For the next twelve months he commanded No. 1690 Bomber Defence Training Flight, flying Hurricanes, then set sail for New Zealand, arriving home at Labour weekend in 1945.

> I came back on the *Andes*. It was a big ship and a fast ship and it broke all records coming from Southampton to Melbourne, and they were all set to do the same from Southampton to Wellington. Because we were going to

Les Munro, 2004. ALISON PARR

arrive on Labour weekend we came across the Tasman half-speed because the wharfies wouldn't work. They refused to work on Labour weekend. There was hell to pay. The troops nearly rebelled and I remember there was a wing commander, OC troops, he had to give an address to the troops because everybody, officers and men alike, were dying to get home and the trip was delayed – I think over two days.

And when we berthed, when the lighter came out carrying old Fred Jones, the Minister of Defence at that time, he was pelted with eggs and God knows what by the returning troops, because he hadn't taken some action against the wharfies. You know, all these fellows coming back, having fought for the country for two, three, four, five years, and these fellows that never left New Zealand refusing to work because it was Labour weekend. Gee, that didn't go down well. I can remember being on the rail watching Jones and company being pelted with eggs and whatever people had saved from breakfast. Yeah. It was really a disappointing end to that trip. Everybody was talking about breaking the record with the ship, and it did until we hit Melbourne, and then everything fell out of it.

In 1948 Les married Betty Hill, a teacher, and the couple had five children. He worked for the State Advances Corporation in land valuation and settlement of returned servicemen for sixteen years before, in 1961, returning to farming until his retirement.

For many years Les was very active in local-body politics, with his work recognised by both the CNZM and QSO. In 1995 he led an official Waitomo District Council delegation to Japan, forging a sister city relationship with the Tatsuno Town Council. Les remains a keen advocate of the peacekeeping role such relationships can play.

I'm a little bit sceptical about trying to commemorate the sacrifices that our men gave in the war, in relation to what those that survived have done to prevent another war. In speeches I have got very provocative. What have we done as survivors to play our part to ensure that another war didn't happen? I cite the sister city movements as playing a major part. Fair enough to go along each Anzac Day service and honour, remember the people that gave their lives. Is that the end of it? Do we stop there? Do we do nothing more about it? I think we should be proactive. Maybe measured against the might of the whole world the role that we could play might be minimal, but at least if everybody did it they might achieve something.

Further reading and web sites

Ambrose, Stephen E., *D-Day, June 6, 1944: The Climactic Battle of World War II*, Simon & Schuster, New York, 1994

Calvocoressi, Peter, Guy Wint and John Pritchard, *The Penguin History of the Second World War*, Penguin Books, London, 1999

Dear, I.C.B., and M.R.D. Foot (eds), *The Oxford Companion to World War II*, Oxford University Press, Oxford, 1995

Edwards, Kenneth, *Operation Neptune*, Collins, London, 1946

Ellis, L.F., et al., *History of the Second World War: Victory in the West, Vol. 1, The Battle of Normandy*, Her Majesty's Stationery Office, London, 1962

Galbreath, Ross, *DSIR: Making Science Work for New Zealand*, Victoria University Press, Wellington, 1998

Hastings, Max, *Overlord: D-Day and the Battle for Normandy*, Vintage, London, 1984

Lambert, Max, *Night after Night: New Zealanders in Bomber Command*, HarperCollins, Auckland, 2005

Mason, W. Wynne, *Prisoners of War*, Department of Internal Affairs, Wellington, 1954

McGibbon, Ian (ed.), *The Oxford Companion to New Zealand Military History*, Oxford University Press, Auckland, 2000

Middlebrook, Martin, and Chris Everitt, *The Bomber Command War Diaries: An Operational Reference Book 1939–1945*, Midland Publishing, Leicester, 1996

Ross, J.M.S., *Royal New Zealand Air Force*, Department of Internal Affairs, Wellington, 1955

Saunders, Hilary St George, *The Royal Air Force, 1939–1945, Volume 3, The Fight is Won*, Her Majesty's Stationery Office, London, 1954

Thomas, David A., *A Companion to the Royal Navy*, Harrap, London, 1988

Thompson, H.L., *New Zealanders with the Royal Air Force*, Department of Internal Affairs, Wellington, Vol. I, 1953, Vol. 2, 1956

Waters, S.D., *The Royal New Zealand Navy*, Department of Internal Affairs, Wellington, 1956

Wells, Kevin W., *An Illustrated History of the New Zealand Spitfire Squadron*, Hutchinson of New Zealand, Auckland, 1984

www.bbc.co.uk/history/war/wwtwo/

www.ddaymuseum.co.uk/

www.nzhistory.net.nz/Gallery/dday/index.html

Index

The names of ships are italicised; illustrations appear in bold.